The Story of
Martha Myers

or Betsy

Barbara Joiner

Barbara Joiner

The Story of
Martha Myers

Barbara Joiner

Birmingham, Alabama

Woman's Missionary Union, SBC
P. O. Box 830010
Birmingham, AL 35283-0010

For more information, visit our Web site at www.wmu.com or call 1-800-968-7301.

Dewey Decimal Classification: 922.6
Subject Headings: MISSIONS—YEMEN
                   MISSIONARY BIOGRAPHY

Scripture quotation marked NASB is taken from the New American Standard Bible®, Copyright © 1960, 1962, 1963, 1968, 1971, 1972, 1973, 1975, 1977, 1995 by The Lockman Foundation. Used by permission.

Design by Janell E. Young
Cover by Cheryl Totty

ISBN: 1-56309-903-9
W054108•0905 •2.5M1

Dedication

I dedicate this book to the Myers family who supported Martha with their whole hearts.

I also dedicate this book to my sister, Nancy Horn Rasco, who pushed me and prayed for me until she went to be with the Father, September 7, 2004. I truly believe she kept right on pushing and praying until I finally completed the book, January 6, 2005.

Contents

Introduction

In 1970, 25-year-old Martha Myers said, "There are times when I am exactly where and doing exactly what the Lord created me for." She had completed her junior year of medical school and was preparing to leave the last of December for 2 months for a receptorship at Jibla Baptist Hospital in Yemen. This trip changed her life. She discovered exactly where God wanted her to be and what He wanted her to do for the rest of her life.

From the comfortable suburbs of Montgomery, Alabama, to the Arabian Peninsula halfway across the world is no easy swap. Yemen is nestled away in the southwest corner of the Arabian Peninsula. It is bordered on the north by Saudi Arabia, on the east by Oman, on the south by the Gulf of Aden, and on the west by the Red Sea. The landscape transitions from narrow sandy beaches along the coast to high plateau meadows and pastures in the west to the mountainous arid terrain leading to the desolate wastelands of the Arabian Desert.

The history of Yemen is fascinating. Around 950 B.C., Yemen and Ethiopia, just across the Red Sea, formed most of the land of Sheba. The Queen of Sheba had her throne in the city of Marib. (Yes, this is the same Queen of Sheba whose trip to see King Solomon is recorded in 1 Kings 10:1–13.) Spice caravans from Yemen began their 1,250-mile trip north to Jerusalem. One of the seven wonders of the ancient world was the great dam near the capital city of Marib. Only the pyramids of Egypt equaled the great dam. It watered fields, orchards, and gardens that were the most beautiful in the world. The dam broke about A.D. 570 and was never rebuilt. Today, Marib is a small town surrounded by sand and desert and rocks.

Islam had been introduced to Yemen around A.D. 628 and quickly spread throughout the country. For over 1,100 years Yemen was ruled by several dynasties of priest kings called imams. During that time they were occupied twice by the Turks. As long as the imams were in power, foreigners were kept out of the country.

In 1962 Imam Ahmed died. The country revolted against having his son take the throne. A republic was begun. At that time, Yemen had been closed to the gospel for more than 1,300 years.

In 1964 Jim and June Young; their four children; and Maria Luisa Hidalgo, a Spanish Baptist contract nurse, moved to Yemen. In March 1965 the temporary Baptist clinic in Ta'izz began seeing patients. During the first month, they saw almost 1,000 patients in over 1,300 clinic visits.

In 1966 they moved to Jibla (located between the capital, Sana'a, and Ta'izz) to build a hospital. They worked in trailers while Jibla Baptist Hospital was being built. They saw 17,000 patients during that year. One year later the new 70-bed Baptist hospital opened its doors.

John D. Hughey, former Foreign Mission Board (now International Mission Board) secretary for Europe and the Middle East said, "That a Baptist witness could be begun in a country almost 100 percent Muslim, and that a hospital could be constructed and equipped under such unfavorable conditions seems beyond the realm of possibility. But the impossible has become a wonderful reality in Yemen."

Three years later Martha arrived to complete a receptorship. She saw beyond the poverty, the hopelessness. She saw the people. She believed that Christianity is communicated best by actions of love, compassion, and service.

Martha returned to the States to finish her senior year of medical school, but her heart remained in Yemen. Psalm 139:13–14 (NASB) declares: "For You formed my inward parts; You wove me in my mother's womb. I will give thanks to You, for I am fearfully and wonderfully made." The psalmist continued to say that the days were ordained when as yet there was not one of them.

Dr. Ira Myers, father of Martha Myers, echoed these verses. "God has a plan for our lives—a plan no one else can fill." And Martha not only knew but also fulfilled God's plan for her life. She "refused to fit a pattern," her father said. "She was unique."

1
The Vagabond Early Years

Martha Myers's advent into the world was unique. At age 19, Ira Lee Myers and Dorothy Will Foust were very much in love. They found it harder to study in separate colleges. With their families' consent, they married. Dorothy transferred from the University of Montevallo to Howard College (now Samford University) in Birmingham, Alabama, where they worked, studied, and borrowed their way through school.

Dorothy graduated with a major in English two weeks before Martha's arrival on March 13, 1945. She was born into a world aflame with war. World War II exhausted America and most of the rest of the globe, but the end was in sight. A few days before Martha's birth the Allies invaded Germany. When Martha was a few days old, American soldiers across the Atlantic were seeing firsthand the horrors of the slave labor camp at Buchenwald when they went in to liberate it. In Asia, Allies were dying on Iwo Jima and Okinawa.

The day before Martha turned 1 month old, Franklin Delano Roosevelt died. He was the only president many Americans could remember, but he would be only a historical figure to Martha. When Martha was 6 months old, too little to join in the celebration, America went wild with joy at Japan's surrender. Christians offered up prayers of thanksgiving to God. Life could go on. For the Myerses, going on included more education for Ira, and a little brother for Martha.

In the fall of 1945, Ira entered the Medical College of Alabama. Dorothy, who had dreamed of being a missionary, accepted a new call: to support her husband and to raise their children in the Lord. In the spring of 1946, they numbered two. Grady was born April 5, 1946.

Martha and Grady attended nursery school while Dorothy worked. The whole family was active in the Norwood Baptist Church. In addition to school and church, they enjoyed a dog, a turtle, and frequent visits to Mom and Pop Myers's farm and Grandmother and Granddaddy's store. Life was good for them, as it was for many families who were making up for lost time during the war years.

During her early preschool days, Martha's medical prowess first became evident. She attempted a blood test by sticking Grady's heel with a safety pin while he was stuck between their bunk bed bars!

Ira completed medical school and the family moved to Seattle, Washington, for his internship. Martha and Grady learned about snow, daylight at bedtime, and raspberry picking. However, the biggest event in Seattle was Dorothy's eight-week hospital stay, which ended another pregnancy, a baby girl. Dorothy had dreamed of a dozen children, but she and Ira decided to look into adoption.

The next year when the Myers family moved to Charleston, West Virginia, Ira and Dorothy brought 13-month-old Stephen Allen into the home. A week later Grady and Martha carried Stephen onto their grandparents' porch as a Christmas surprise.

Martha loved first grade, which she had started in Charleston; but after Christmas the family moved to Buffalo, New York, for 6 months.

After Buffalo, they were off to Boston where Ira got his master's degree in public health at Harvard University. Behind their house in the woods was a pond, with a steep hill leading down to it—perfect for sledding! Kids went through the yard with skates over their shoulders.

They loved that place and met salamanders, tadpoles, and snakes. Ira even introduced the children to the anatomy of an etherized frog. Martha couldn't see the anatomy for the tears! She claimed it would have been all right if her daddy had sewn him back up and let him go. This may have turned Martha away from medicine, at least temporarily.

While in Massachusetts, the family went to court to finalize Steve's adoption. Not long after, on a sightseeing trip to Mount Rushmore an incident occurred that convinced them that Steve was especially meant for the Myers family.

Steve had been sleeping in the back car window when he began having convulsions. Ira directed the car to the nearest town to a small hospital. They emerged hours later with Steve, sleeping in a borrowed blanket. He had had his first grand mal seizure, probably related to meningitis, which he had had at 6 months of age.

Seizures were well controlled with Dilantin and the Myerses have been able to provide the medical, physical, spiritual, and noncoercive educational care Steve has needed. His humor, hard work, and quiet companionship are priceless to the entire family.

Church life was highly varied from city to city from 1949 to 1953. Martha admitted that she hardly remembered the Seattle church. She did recall that as the Myerses moved out, the first Southern Baptist church was established in town. Ira and Dorothy donated their piano to the church. Martha had taken piano lessons for several months before she was 5. When they left the Northwest, good-bye piano!

A warm church greeted the family in Charleston, West Virginia. Martha sang in the children's choir and her first hymn with the congregation was "Have Thine Own Way, Lord."

In Buffalo the children liked the church that served orange juice and cookies, but the parents chose the one with Sunday night services.

During the 5-year sojourn up North, Ira and Dorothy were especially mindful of religious education in their home. The children heard Wild West stories of Old Testament wars and learned Bible verses at bedtime and tried to repeat them at breakfast.

In the 1950s families were growing, and income for many Americans was growing too. People bought cars, televisions, and convenience foods. President Eisenhower was a comforting presence in the midst of the cold war.

The 1950s were good for the Myerses, too. In 1954 the parents were excited to be moving to Atlanta—to Southern Baptist territory! Martha's father took employment with the Centers for Disease Control in Atlanta. The children were awed by the friendliness of kids their own age and amazed by the church activities: Sunbeams, choir, Sunday School, Training Union, Vacation Bible School, as well as church services. They had found a wonderful church home—First Baptist Church of Avondale Estates.

Sometimes there were special treats like movies instead of Sunday night church. Martha was a Primary and they got out of Training Union early to get a front row seat at the first movie: *Oil Town, U.S.A.* She recalled it was a good movie with lots of action, conflict, and music. At the end, the screen characters sat listening to George Beverly Shea's recording of "The Love of God."

During those moments, Martha experienced God's claim on her own life. She began to cry and was surprised that nobody else was moved to tears—not Grady or her best friend, Diane Barber. She went down front, but she and a boy named Johnny Keith were lost amid the Primary and Junior kids crowding the front rows. Their decisions went unannounced.

Afterward, however, the pastor, Victor A. Greene, found them and prayed with them.

Dr. and Mrs. Myers asked the pastor to their home for a conference with their daughter before Martha presented herself to the church. Soon after she was baptized.

Third grade was a busy time. Martha graduated from Sunbeams to Girls' Auxiliary. Alas! They discovered their Brownie troop also met on GA® day. They informed the Brownie leader that they wanted to be Brownies, but that GA came first.

Brownies was changed to Tuesdays. Another afternoon was for piano. She had to start from middle C since she had been without a piano or lessons for 4 years.

Church rolls were swelling and missions programs of many denominations were growing. Martha and her best friend in third grade, a Methodist girl named Linda Ott, both caught the fever. Linda joined Martha in planning to quit school as soon as the law allowed in order to go to China as missionaries. In the meantime, they tried to witness to the bullies in their class, and tried to start a Bible study during recess. Little did Martha know how many years of schooling she would have before her before she could become a missionary!

When Dorothy Myers became pregnant again, she and Ira used that opportunity to add to the children's understanding of the facts of life, to which they already had been introduced by eight Samoyed puppies.

When eight-pound Joanna Lynn arrived, she received a lot of Martha's attention. In fact, Grady was disgusted that he could no longer get her to play cowboys in the woods or hunt bullets and snakes in the Civil War trench behind their house.

Life was changing for Martha, for the entire Myers family. The vagabond years were over. They were headed for Montgomery, Alabama, where Ira and Dorothy would put down family roots.

2
Putting Down Roots in Montgomery, Alabama

In 1955 the Myers family moved to Montgomery, Alabama, where Dr. Myers became administrative officer of the Alabama State Health Department.

Martha mourned leaving her church in Atlanta, her friends, and her secret boyfriend. But her biggest regret was leaving Linda Ott. They consoled themselves with the assurance that *Apple,* their code word for the Holy Spirit, was in this.

Montgomery was not as large as Atlanta, and was located on the flat plains of southern Alabama. The Alabama River flowed nearby. When the nearby cotton fields were ready for harvest, the bursting bolls made it look as if snow had fallen. Spanish moss draped the limbs of trees like lacy gray shawls around the shoulders of so many old ladies. Winters were short and mild. Summers were long and ferocious. It was a different world from Boston, or even Atlanta. It was to become home.

The family joined Dalraida Baptist Church, which had a strong missions program. Again Martha was part of the Girls' Auxiliary (GA). Other GA friends shared her medical passions. In the sixth grade, Bonnie, Barbara, and she talked incessantly about medicine. They would read and bring new words to the group to be defined: words like *enema* or *pneumoencephalomyelography*. (Guess who brought that word!)

Martha was sure that the Lord was calling her into medical missions. Her parents, however, cautioned her not to confuse her own ideas with the Lord's will. She did, at that time, surrender her education—no matter how long—to the Lord.

One of Martha's delights during this time was her little sister, Joanna. They were always close. Martha claimed that 9 years' difference in age made for admiration on both parts without competition.

In addition, Martha made "for-life" friends in Montgomery. Listen to what a few of them remember about her.

Ellen Rooke

Ellen Rooke proudly claims Martha as her very best friend. "I met Martha when I first attended Dalraida Baptist Church in Montgomery. She was my first friend. We were in everything together at church—choir; Girls' Auxiliary; and, later, Young Woman's Auxiliary.

"We were together a lot. When Martha went to college, we stayed friends. When she became a missionary, we stayed friends.

"I helped her pack her trunks when she left for Yemen. Always she packed more for the people in Yemen than for herself.

"When Martha came home for short furloughs, I was often her driver when she was invited to speak. I was honored to do that. She was my dear friend always. I prayed for her faithfully.

"One regret," Ellen admits. "We promised each other we would not leave YWA until we received our white Bibles. White Bibles were always presented to new brides. Unfortunately, neither of us were presented a white Bible!"

Linda Cox Baker

"The Myers family joined Dalraida Baptist Church 6 months after my family joined. Martha was about 2 years older with only one grade ahead of me in school. I was quiet, bashful, and shy. Martha was, however, in her own little world."

Linda remembers being in GA, choir, and other church activities with Martha. She remembers a girl who was both kind and smart. "Martha was always helping anyone who needed her," Linda recalls.

"She loved science. When we went to camp she told us about the fungus on trees, pointed out poison ivy to us. She also delighted in finding a dead snake which she immediately dissected and checked out!"

Nothing fazed Martha—not having her pajama legs sewed up, not having a frog in her bed. Linda claims Martha's strength came from her family. "They had family altar. They had Bible reading and prayer and they talked. The children discussed things with the parents." Being down-to-earth helped Martha avoid vanity for her accomplishments, which were many.

"She was talented. She could play the piano, she could sing, and she was a soloist. She was fluent in Spanish and won spelling bees.

"If anybody needed help, she'd help. She was an inspiration to all of us. I could tell her anything and she could share with me. Both of us enjoyed time together to relax and rest. We loved beach time.

"Our friendship did not end when Martha went to Yemen. My prayers went with her. When she came home on her brief furloughs, if she needed a driver, I was glad to go. She loved my Death by Chocolate cookies. We shared many of those cookies."

One of the last trips Linda and Martha took together was to New Orleans Baptist Theological Seminary. Martha spoke to a class planning to go to Yemen. The following morning, Linda claims, they went wild—they went down to the French Quarter and ate beignets at the Café du Monde before returning home!

Vicky Smith Davis

Vicky's friendship with Martha began when her father, Dr. John L. Smith, became pastor of Dalraida Baptist Church in the early 1960s. The girls became friends because of church and its emphasis on missions. Vicky claims that Martha was a humble servant completely possessed by Jesus.

"In GA we learned the Star Ideals," says Vicky. "They epitomized the life and walk of Martha Myers. GA taught us to pray, to read our Bibles, to serve the Lord. Particularly we learned to accept the challenge of the Great Commission. We were intrigued with our studies of foreign missions. Little did we know that God had already begun a good work and was calling our Martha to be a 'real live' missionary!"

Vicky suspected Martha spent a lot of time reading her father's medical journals. "She shared bits of medical information with us." One night Vicky was spending the night at Martha's house. They had both washed their hair and were preparing for bed when Vicky realized the window air conditioner would blow directly on them.

"We'll catch a cold, maybe even pneumonia!" Vicky wailed. Martha immediately informed her that colds weren't caught in that manner, and launched into a detailed but clear medical explanation of cold germs. Vicky never worries about her wet head anymore.

Vicky knew about one of Martha's extracurricular activities because she was enlisted as a helper. Working with Elizabeth Church, a specialist with 4-year-olds, Martha taught Beginners in Bible school. The Sunday School Board (now LifeWay Christian Resources) asked Elizabeth to conduct a Bible school for the children at Pineview Manor, a private home for mentally and physically handicapped children one-half mile from their church.

They found a class of Down syndrome children; a girl in a wheelchair with cerebral palsy; a 40-year-old woman with severe cerebral palsy on a stretcher; and Greg and Emily, whose limitations seemed to be entirely physical and environmental.

After the Bible school ended, Elizabeth and Martha continued a weekly Sunday School. During this time, Martha enlisted Vicky. Actually, they were doing Saturday School. Interest grew and the girls discovered they did not have all the spiritual answers. Martha approached her pastor, Vicky's father, about helping. Dr. Smith agreed to come.

One of their students, Emily, wanted to go to church. Martha found a way to get her to Dalraida. Dorothy Myers, from whom Martha acquired the gift of getting involved, was Emily's first Sunday School teacher. Emily soon made her profession of faith and was baptized.

Junior years' summers were times for GA camp, meeting new girls, talking to "real, live" missionaries, lying in a top bunk listening to vesper chimes, and wondering about God and His plan for Martha's life.

In 1960 Martha entered Lee High School in Montgomery. She claimed her high school years were comfortable. A traumatic B in algebra one six weeks caused Grady to exclaim, "Maybe she is normal!"

She formed deep attachments with several teachers. One was a 23-year-old red-headed Unitarian biologist, Miss Marlar. One of Martha's heartbreaks was Miss Marlar's refusal to visit the church, even for Martha's coronation as Queen Regent in GA or her solo in a Christmas cantata.

Too soon high school ended. She knew she'd miss her students whom she had tutored in Spanish, art, music, and arithmetic one summer. (The children came from the private grammar school where her mother taught fifth grade.) She'd miss working with Junior GAs, the two boys she had tried to teach to play the piano, and the children of Pineview Manor. How did she do it all? God only knows. He was preparing her for more and more and more.

3
Spreading Her Wings at Howard

In the fall of 1963 Martha began her college career at a Baptist school, Howard College (now Samford University). She had planned to attend the University of Alabama and major in biology. Her first career choice was educational missions, with medical missions as second choice. Meeting with Howard College biologists and a scholarship offer from Leslie Wright, president of the college, changed her mind.

The Howard College campus was nestled on a low rolling hillside of Homewood, a suburb of Birmingham. In those years Birmingham was a steel-making giant, and the air often reeked from the steel mills. Howard College, however, was a green oasis of beauty.

Although Martha loved teaching and enjoyed assisting in labs in biology, zoology, botany, comparative anatomy, and microbiology, she could never schedule education classes. God has a way of closing doors.

Not only did Martha enjoy her work, but she also wanted to help with her college education. While her family appreciated her offer, they assured her it was not absolutely necessary. Dr. Myers had been elected Alabama's state health officer. He was responsible for all state health programs including drug abuse policing, air and water pollution control, Medicaid, and health legislation.

He was in a unique position to preach to youth groups, churches, and pastors. His salary growth stayed at least one jump ahead of his family's needs.

In college Martha continued throwing herself into many activities. She was editor of the literary magazine, president of the dorm council, president of the biology society, member of the A Cappella Choir, and an active Southern Baptist.

Alabama in the early 1960s was a cauldron of racial tensions. George Wallace had defied President Kennedy when Wallace stood in the schoolhouse door at the University of Alabama in June 1963. At Wallace's inauguration he had declared, "Segregation today, segregation tomorrow, segregation forever!" There were marches and sit-ins and boycotts. In Birmingham fire hoses and attack dogs were used on black demonstrators. The eyes of the nation and the world were on Martha's home state. How did she feel about all this?

Oddly enough, her journal says nothing about the turmoil going on around her. Her friends and loved ones have concluded that Martha was so focused on God's particular call on her life, she had no time and attention left over for all the other things going on.

During her freshman year, Martha was a member of Alabama's largest church (at the time), Dawson Memorial in Birmingham. The following year she joined Westside Baptist Church in Wylam, a community between two steel mills. She visited the church to play the organ during a revival. It was Martha's first time to play one! She recognized meetable needs of the small church and community.

During the rest of her Howard College days, Martha taught Intermediates in Sunday School at Westside. If no one came, she would save the lesson for the afternoon, round up a group of seven, and teach them in someone's living room.

She played the piano for children's choir and attempted to teach some of the kids a few elementals about piano. She picked up so many dirty kids and examined their dogs, cats, possums, alligators, ducks, and rabbits that she had a hard time wearing a dry-cleaned dress to church.

Martha was not the only college student drawn to Wylam. She always involved others when there was a need. Some of Martha's brigade were Mike Bristow, Allen Hill, Vicky Smith, and Judy Cadenhead. She also enlisted Marcia Gwin Wright. Martha needed someone to play the piano at Westside while she went on choir tour to Europe with the A Cappella Choir. Marcia agreed to go.

When Martha returned from the tour, Marcia's life had already changed. Martha suggested she continue going to Westside. So she joined the church and for the rest of her Howard College days enjoyed singing, playing the piano occasionally, and witnessing to people in the community.

Another of the Wylam crew that Martha enlisted was her Dalraida friend, Vicky Smith Davis, also a Howard College student. The church purchased a small used portable organ and Martha recruited Vicky to be volunteer organist. All of these young college people were a formidable crew. They blessed the church and the church blessed them.

Marcia remembers that Sundays were special. In time they had a Howard group that rode from school together to Wylam. They learned to love the people and were loved in return. The church people welcomed the college students with open arms and open doors. Almost every Sunday they were invited home to dinner at the homes of the Moores, the McCains, the Wheatleys, the Millers, the Beavers, the Yarbroughs, Ms. Vance, the Smiths, or the Skinners.

Marcia continues by saying Martha was greatly loved by the people in Wylam. She had a great capacity for loving people, listening to their concerns, their needs, their stories, and for sharing Christ's message in such an easy, nonthreatening manner. She always seemed so mature, contented, and happy—never materialistic, selfish, or pretentious. She always had a tender, sweet, smiling expression on her face—a true reflection of the beautiful person inside.

Martha was the same on campus. She was the role model, the leader, the medical advisor, and the "wise counsel." (If that all sounds too good to be true, I can only quote those who knew Martha best: "That was Martha!")

But Westside and school did not take all of Martha's time. During college years, Martha served two summers as a Home Mission Board (now North American Mission Board) summer missionary. In 1966 she went to Frontier Baptist Association in the Buffalo-Rochester, New York, area.

"It was one of the richest seasons of my life," wrote Martha in her journal.

Four worked together: Martha, Jimmy, Mike, and Nella under the supervision of the area director, Chuck Magruder. He impressed on them the potential of the area and the opportunities. The summer missionaries had a warm companionship in common purpose and prayer. The highlights were surveying, revivals, a victorious Bible school in a mission that was about to close, a Polish Bible school and revival, a park VBS, beginning new missions, personal witnessing to adults, friendship with young people in the association, and the first associational youth camp.

Others of Martha's generation were dropping out of school, experimenting with drugs, joining communes, protesting the Vietnam War, or trying to find themselves through Eastern religions or the Peace Corps. Martha's journey of self-awareness was taken in the company of her Savior. The more she served Him, the more she knew who and what she was.

Those summer missions experiences helped her along the way. Maybe it was the little girl hospitalized because of a neglected ingrown toenail, the 3-year-old with a splinter in her infected hand, the girl with gastroenteritis (upset stomach) at camp, the softball hero with extensive abrasions—probably it was all of these that helped Martha know. When she returned from Buffalo, Martha told her mother she was going to medical school.

Dorothy had always told Martha that she would be kicked out of the nest after college. Now she replied, "Well, I don't guess you've heard, but your father just got a raise. I guess that's what the Lord intended it to be used for."

Martha applied to the University of Alabama School of Medicine, also located in Birmingham. She was accepted by the admissions committee, despite Ds in organic chemistry and advanced calculus.

Yes, Grady, she was getting more normal all the time!

4
Making It in Medical School

Things in Montgomery were changing, too. In their younger years Grady and Martha had been good playing buddies, but as they grew older their interests diverged. Grady liked sports cars, popular radio, and beekeeping. He finished Troy State University with a business degree, joined the National Guard, and came back from service ready to settle down. He married and started a family while Martha was up to her ears in medical school.

Steve graduated from high school with his seizures well controlled. Although of normal intelligence, he had been slow to speak as a toddler, and he was still a quiet fellow. Martha and he had a special bond. She declared that his humor, hard work, and quiet companionship were priceless. His shared confidences were treasured.

When Martha left for college, Joanna cried herself to sleep for weeks. When Joanna had arrived in 1954, the two Myers girls found soul mates. "Our hearts are alike," declares Joanna. Her heartache at Martha's leaving eased when she discovered she could go and hang out with her big sister during spring break and summer vacations. Joanna found it exhausting, however, to try and keep up with her!

As for Martha, she described Joanna as a compassionate Christian, almost too serious. Growing up in the tumultuous 1960s and early 1970s, she had seen drug deaths, pregnancies, attempted suicides, and cancer deaths in her classmates. On the other hand, she was the only real teenager in the Myers family. She liked trying new hairstyles, followed fashions, and loved doing things with a group. She adored her big sister.

Meanwhile, brilliant Martha, who could carry impossible loads in classes and outside classes, was having trouble dealing with medical school. "It was a humbling experience," she admitted. She found herself inadequate to cope with anatomy and biochemistry and drowning in the material. But she hung on and kept on. She continued going to Westside Baptist Church, but was not able to serve as actively as she had in college.

Relief was soon to come. Her sophomore year was more clinically oriented and study more rewarding. During the free quarter, Martha worked in immunology research with Dr. Max Cooper. She was excited by the major revelations coming through combined studies in patients and animal models. Martha had no idea how valuable this study would be to her in later years. In Yemen she would direct the community immunization program—a cooperative effort between Jibla Baptist Hospital, UNICEF, and the Yemeni government.

When Martha reached her junior year of medical school, her joy knew no bounds—real, live patients! She was so excited, enthusiastic, ignorant, and eager to learn that she didn't sleep more than four or five hours a night the whole first month on the ward. This was the beginning of a lifelong habit, one which concerned those around her. The chief resident of Mobile General Hospital even ordered Martha out of the hospital one night. To defend herself, she explained that since the hospital didn't have sleeping quarters, when she was busy with renal acidosis, malaria, or staying up until 2:00 A.M. to watch a just-resuscitated patient, she would walk to her car and go home or curl up on a stretcher or the sofa in the house-staff library. This same habit of either going home at odd hours or sleeping at the hospital carried over into her life in Yemen.

While in school, Martha learned so much about medicine and so much about people as she watched dramas unfold around her. Some of it was inspiring, but some of it was sobering.

Her intern resuscitated a man in heart failure whose wife wanted him dead. In fact, the wife returned the next day with her hair fixed for his funeral.

She watched a man who had fallen out of bed five hours earlier die as she was feeding him supper.

After a five-day fight they lost a 54-year-old father of four; but they saved a guy who, if not protected from himself, would eat salt and narcotics and be at death's door again within a week.

At the University of Alabama School of Medicine, Martha explained, students have a close association with the house staff and most attending physicians. They teach those students a lot and they know them well. Gerald New told Martha she was so stubborn she'd argue with a door! Martha defended herself by saying she entered medical school because she related better to individuals than to groups and the patient was the center of her learning. Her patients were hers, to listen to their family problems as well as their chief complaint, to explain their symptoms and answer their questions about tests and work-ups.

Pamela, a 6-year-old African American girl with biliary atresia, was one of Martha's patients. Pamela's condition prevented the bile ducts in her liver from working, and gradually the build-up of bile damaged the liver. When she left the hospital, Martha and her roommate, Lynita Caudill, took Pamela and three siblings to the circus. It was the only place besides the hospital that Pam had ever been. Three weeks later, Martha attended her inevitable funeral, the result of liver failure.

Georgia, a 44-year-old African American woman with everything but TB and diabetes, was another patient belonging to Martha. At five days post-op, she complained of being short of breath and short on digoxin, a heart drug. They found her right middle and lower lung lobes completely collapsed. They coughed her to recovery.

Three weeks later Georgia complained "that medicine is getting to me." Her pulse was 39, but in the next few minutes she arrested from hyperkalemia (too much potassium). Martha began pushing on her sternum. Georgia recovered enough to complain at the beginning of an exhausting three-hour resuscitation, "Hey, cut that out! You're going to break my ribs."

Georgia taught Martha about her way of life, the clinic, and the indigent patient's view of clinic care.

Unless you have a medical background, dear reader, you did not understand many words or conditions. But couldn't you feel all that Martha was learning? She was becoming Dr. Martha!

5

Receptorship
Revelation

Her medical school years were flying by. In 1970, shortly before Martha's last year in medical school, she was given the opportunity for some hands-on experience on the missions field. The Caduceus Club, alumni of the University of Alabama School of Medicine, provided funds for her to work in Nigeria. This was not politically permissible due to civil war in that West African nation.

Martha met with Edna Frances Dawkins of the Foreign Mission Board (now International Mission Board) to consider possibly going to Gaza or Rhodesia (now Zimbabwe). Edna Frances talked of Yemen. Martha was captivated.

The receptorship program of the Foreign Mission Board gave medical workers who felt called to medical missions the opportunity to have experience in overseas settings. For Martha the 2 months she spent in Jibla Baptist Hospital in Yemen cemented her call to medical missions and specifically her call to Yemen. What a revelation!

Martha found much that was fascinating about Yemen. There were mosques and sultans' palaces, and little mountain villages almost inaccessible to travelers. Some people still lived in ancient mud buildings, with their animals stabled on the ground floor while the family occupied the upper floors.

When she reached Jibla, she found a city rich in antiquities and ruins, with arched bridges spanning the two rivers that ran nearby. She also found the Baptist hospital.

When she reached the hospital, Dr. David Dorr said, "I don't know what you want to do about the call schedule, but the other receptors have wanted to be on call every night unless they were out of town."

Martha said, "I had heard that John Potts, receptor to Gaza, 1970, was on call every third night." She thought, "When do I wash my hair?" But the Jibla climate was more favorable than humid Alabama! How could she refuse?

"Of course, in the clinic you will see only women and children," Dr. Dorr continued. "In the evenings, you will see whoever comes as an emergency."

Martha remembered that she may have protested because in school, they took whoever came by turn, male or female. The culture of Yemen was very different from Alabama, however.

She freely admitted that she didn't know much as a senior student but that God graciously gave her wisdom to know when to holler for help.

And there was plenty of reason to need help. Yemen was and is a poor country. It did not enjoy the huge oil revenues of neighboring Arab states, though oil exploitation increased in the 1990s. Yemen is twice as big as Wyoming, but less than 3 percent of the land is suitable for growing crops. Most of the country is desert, with some fertile soil in the west, and the vast majority of people eke out a living in farming or herding. In 1970 there were few paved roads and rampant illiteracy.

Martha learned that life expectancy was low and infant mortality was high. Women especially suffered from lack of medical care, harsh work, and often poor treatment by husbands and families. Thanks to her medical colleagues, she also learned a lot about medicine. She enjoyed balanced freedom and direction from the missionary doctors. Dr. Jim Young coached her in clinic, let her admit and treat a man with an amoebic hepatic abscess, then showed her how to manage this as an outpatient. He showed her how to remove bladder stones, which are common even in the children.

She assisted in a variety of surgical procedures. The vesicovaginal fistula, preventable by reasonable obstetric care, is the reason for admission of a large percentage of women. This fistula, or hole in the bladder, is caused by difficult or prolonged labor. The fistula causes leaking in the bladder, and the urine odor makes the woman unclean. Many of these fistula patients were divorced and sent back home to live with their parents. Often they would be put in a back room where their presence would not remind the family of their shame.

The fistula requires fairly lengthy hospitalization, but when corrected, results in a dramatically changed life. Dr. Young and Dr. Dorr were exultant with the successful repair. One of Martha's victories was seeing the lesion become obsolete after she learned to do the repair. This surgery literally gave her patients a new lease on life!

Martha readily admitted frustrations: treating a boy with probable TB meningitis; giving a baby with heart failure and pneumonia oxygen straight from the tank; referring a sick young man to the TB hospital in Ta'izz; leaving Amin, who probably needed a mitral valve replacement; trying to communicate God's sufficiency to a man who could hardly breathe; telling a mastectomy patient that her baby had died (from severe dehydration secondary to gastroenteritis, probably due to diet change); managing a man in shock without central venous pressure; losing a young man whose GI bleed was probably a result of schistosomiasis and cirrhosis.

There were victories, too. She watched Russ Roland, an internist, successfully manage a fellow with renal failure without lab work. A boy was cured of congestive heart failure and hypertension by removal of a malfunctioning kidney.

The successes as well as the frustrations were striking in a referral hospital in a land crying for preventive medicine and someone to handle emergencies.

The Yemen Mission gave Martha much. Maria Luisa Hidalgo, the first nurse in Yemen, shared the history of the work in the country and the loneliness she had felt when her father died in Spain. Johnnie Brasswell let her help teach the nursing students.

Tea, hot chocolate, and homemade hamburger buns and peanut butter were shared in the single nurses' homes. The Egyptian and Swedish nurses shared their culture and Christian fellowship. Ethne Stainer, a contract nurse from Australia, taught her a lot about prayer as she prayed for her Yemeni co-workers in the operating room or the pharmacy every day. She grew close to the doctors' wives and to their children when they visited on vacation.

The Yemeni women, however, made the biggest impact on Martha. She heard them whisper among themselves, "She came just for us." Martha purposed to return to them.

6
Getting Ready to Return to Yemen

When Martha returned to the US, she went back to Birmingham to medical school—her senior year. Even though she felt it went slowly, she completed the year and received her MD in 1971.

In July of 1971 she began her internship at the University of South Alabama Medical Center in Mobile, serving a rotating internship. During a year of general surgery, Martha primarily cared for emergency and trauma patients. She had major responsibilities to one or several attending doctors during three- to four-month rotations in neurosurgery; ear, nose and throat; plastic surgery, and cardiovascular surgery.

In the fall of 1972, some comments of Roberta Kells Dorr (the wife of Yemen's Dr. David Dorr) confirmed to Martha that she needed more training in obstetrics, gynecology, and pediatrics.

During a six-month residency, Martha discovered that neonatology had changed drastically in only two years. After 6 months of obstetrics, she could do a good cesarean section but was not prepared to handle complications.

She trained under superior doctors: Dr. Mendenhall, an excellent obstetrician, who was competent, wise, and cared about the patients' welfare. He also taught Martha a

lot about cancer and dying patients. In Dr. Billy Hightower, she found the same high regard for life, technical
skill, and honesty that characterized Dr. John Kirklin. Dr.
Hightower shared his patients with her, taught her technique, and much about patient management.

She was soaking up medical expertise during both
internship and residency, but in her journal she records
her heart cry. "I was spiritually famished when I reached
Mobile. My personal devotional life had suffered in medical school and our church had an immature pastor and I
had heard nothing new in months." She wanted to be
active in a neighborhood church, but friends insisted that
she visit Dauphin Way Baptist Church.

After a concert of sacred music by a baritone who sang
everything from opera to "Amazing Grace" and back, and
after a brief sermon by Dr. Jaroy Weber, the handwriting
was readable on the wall and she joined. Any church that
loved that type of preaching and singing had just what she
needed.

Later that year, Dr. Weber talked about people who
"ate only when they went to church." Martha decided
that described her life in Birmingham; and with no food at
church, she was starved.

Dauphin Way had an active single adult group, but
Martha's call schedule interfered with social activities and
regular Sunday School attendance. Choir became her
major fellowship group and Doug Scott, the minister of
music, with his sermonettes and Scripture-filled music,
was a special spiritual leader. Doug's secretary, Peggy
Shoemaker, adopted Martha and she usually ate dinner
with her and her five children.

Though Martha was devoted to God's calling, she was
still a young woman with a young woman's natural interests. One Saturday, Peggy's washing machine was broken
and Martha had to make a trip to the coin laundry. She
met a guy named Jim who asked what she was reading.

She told him, "a book about prayer," which interested him rather than turned him off. When he agreed to go to Sunday School the next day, she had to be on time!

A few months later Jeanette, her next-door neighbor, asked about their singles group. They went to Sunday School together the next morning. A tall guy named John Ladner played the piano. A blonde college graduate, Kathy Barnett, joined the church that day and the girls invited her to eat seafood. The girls wanted to go after church fellowship, which Martha's schedule had not previously allowed, and they went. John had talked with the singles about the importance of a personal quiet time and he shared with Martha about this at the fellowship.

Kathy asked about a Bible study and they discovered one had been started at John's apartment. They were studying Genesis. Martha was now an OB resident, a member of a team, and had more free time. The Bible study became the week's highlight.

John had the gift of teaching. Martha declared she never failed to learn from him. She also admitted that one reason she was so strongly attracted to him was that he provided spiritual leadership for her. But no permanent relationships appeared on the horizon.

When Alabama Woman's Missionary Union held its annual meeting at Dauphin Way in Mobile in 1972, four women from First Baptist, Columbiana, attended the meeting. One of the women, Barbara Joiner, had fallen in love with Yemen before Martha had. She and Martha had become great friends with that common love. Martha insisted the four women stay with her. Edna Verchot, Bennie Holcombe, Ann Foster, and Barbara treasured that experience. Edna Verchot prayed every day for Martha when she went to Yemen. Bennie never forgot gathering up the bedspread laden with sample medicines and depositing it in a corner of the room so that the four women could go to bed.

And Barbara found a doctor for migrant camp. Since 1969 First Baptist, Columbiana, had gone to Baldwin County, just across from Mobile Bay, and ministered in migrant camps. Every year Martha brought her little black bag and went into the camps. She was a missionary to migrants years before going to Yemen.

Martha's final journal entry before leaving Mobile in June of 1976 is excited and honest and very much the heart of an exceptional Christian young woman. She wrote, "I think I will be able to help. I have no delusions about giving total patient care but I would like to be part of the team in Yemen. I think I am at a level of training where I can both be of service and continue to learn. I have found that you can't save every patient, even in the medical center. . . . I have worked under authority and under restrictions in evangelism.

"I realize my helplessness without Christ. He is my Savior and my Lord and I want Him to be my life. I believe in the power of prayer and He is teaching me to pray but I recognize this as a largely untapped resource.

"I have considered Paraguay, Gaza, Korea, Nigeria, but I have no directional leading other than Yemen. If Doctor Young and the Foreign Mission Board will have me, I am ready to go and am in the process of applying to seminary."

7
Dotting All the I's, Crossing All the T's, and Learning Arabic

Martha Crystal Myers, MD, was commissioned as a career missionary by the Southern Baptist Foreign Mission Board in 1976. She headed immediately to Kansas City, Missouri, for the required 1 year of training for medical doctors at Midwestern Baptist Theological Seminary. Even though she was going to Yemen as a doctor, she had to take some basic seminary classes before going on the field.

Anything else? Did she want to become proficient in Arabic, the language of Yemen? Of course, and she did become fluent in their language. Off she went to London, England, for intensive study. While most of her generation was learning disco dancing, Martha was learning a Middle Eastern language. While her American counterparts were sitting in avocado-green kitchens eating fondue and wearing double-knit polyester, Martha was learning to have English tea and worship in a different style.

She had been faithful about writing in her journal; however, letter writing was not her thing. A few remnants of letters have survived. From two of them we get a glimpse into her London days. We also see evidence of her love for children and her willingness to embrace a lifestyle different from what she had always known.

The first letter written to Mom, Sissy, and Aunt Mabel is dated January 31, 1978, and says, "Happy New Year!" Typical Martha! She claimed she arrived in London about 25 minutes ahead of schedule due to a good tailwind.

Martha let them know she was attending church: "I have been attending Westminster Chapel, where G. Campbell Morgan used to preach. The pastor is now Dr. R. T. Kendall, who is a graduate of Southern Seminary and a Southern Baptist. He is a very good preacher and I have really appreciated this.

"I have visited Spurgeon's Tabernacle which is also Baptist. The sermon was good. The hymns have different tunes and some are different altogether, but I think I am getting used to that. I have not gotten used to hearing good evangelistic sermons with no invitation given!

"But I have been going to the chapel enough to see that God is still in the soul-winning business even when the worship forms are different.

"Last Sunday, instead of going home to study, I stayed and ate lunch with a single girl named Rosemarie. Many families bring lunch and eat together after church. There are at least four stoves in the kitchen."

Letter 1 also thanks them for her Christmas gifts: "Mom, thanks for the Christmas gifts. I think they are a very nice selection. The heirlooms I really do treasure. Even little things like what I wear remind me of home and specific people and friends.

"I have worn my little green slippers in bed some, but usually if I warm up the pillows in front of the gas heater (that is coin-operated!) and jump in bed with them under four blankets, I stay warm until morning.

"Am enclosing toilet tissue sample from London airport and local crossword puzzle in English-English.

"See you at Joanna's wedding."

The only other "found" letter was to Aunt Maude and was dated February 4, 1978.

"Happy Birthday! I'm afraid this card will be a few days late getting to you!

"Aunt Maude, I wish I could take you to church with me. I have been going to an independent evangelical church a couple of blocks from Buckingham Palace where Queen Elizabeth lives. The preacher is a Southern Baptist from Kentucky. He came to England to study theology at Oxford and a year ago today he preached his first sermon at Westminster Chapel. He was their interim pastor, but they asked him to stay.

"There are many things different about this church. They have a big pipe organ, two circular balconies, and no choir. The preacher goes to the vestry after the sermon instead of standing at the door to shake hands. They do not have an invitation hymn. After the last hymn everyone sits down and prays for a few minutes.

"We have learned a lot [in language classes]. We learned about 400 words the first month. The teachers are pleased with our progress. I have read about four verses from John's Gospel. I think that is a good place to start because he uses many simple words—even though it is not a simple book. . . . Some old fairy tales have been translated into Arabic. I have two children's books in Arabic: *The Little Red Hen* and *The Grains of Wheat*. I can take [them] with me when I go to Yemen and read them to the children.

"One nice custom this English church has is tea (with fresh bread and butter and cakes) before the Bible study on Friday night. Also, after the Sunday night service, they have tea or coffee or "biscuits" (which are really cookies) for 10 cents after church. It gives people a chance to visit and has been real helpful for a new person like me to meet people.

"I hope you are well. Soon the winter will be over in Alabama. I know you will look forward to being able to have the front door open.

"I got a letter today from Dr. Young in Yemen. He thinks it would be a good thing for me to start work at the hospital in May and spend three days a week in the hospital and three days studying. I could learn the Yemeni Arabic and they have some tapes and books from one course we are using here. Later I could come back for a short course."

Two matters in the letters need to be addressed. In letter 1, Martha promised to see everybody at Joanna's wedding. In fact, she was Joanna's maid of honor. She made it the day before the March 25 wedding—just in time for the bridesmaids luncheon. In fact, she walked in and her mother said, "We can now begin the bridesmaids luncheon. Martha is here!"

In letter 2 she writes about receiving a letter from Dr. Young asking her to come to Yemen in May. She began her work there on May 1, 1978.

8
Yemen—at Last

How to explain those early years in Yemen? Martha no longer kept her journal. She was too busy. And she *never* wrote letters. But others wrote letters! Letters dated from the 1960s to 2004, which included 14 cards and letters from Martha Myers!

One card was dated 1977 and was from Midwestern Seminary and demanded a report from migrant camp. It was the first she'd missed in years.

She also reported she'd passed the first month so "these guys"—the faculty—"know what grace is."

Another gift from God was posted March 1978 and was from the Polyglot School (UK) Ltd., London, England! In this letter Martha announced, "Behold I come quickly and should be on Montgomery turf by 24/March for sister Joanna's wedding on 25/March." Unfortunately, Martha's letter arrived two weeks after the wedding.

The next card was dated June 30, 1978, from Yemen. She apologized for having been there 2 months without having written.

She also asked for prayer for the hospital staff, saying, "It's a real stress to have new people—at least me!"

She also stated the highlight of the week was the Arabic preaching. Every Sunday night one of the hospital staff preached in Arabic to all the staff. Already her studies were clicking in.

And she was going full force in the hospital.

The next word from Yemen concerning Martha was nearly a year later in a Christmas card from Jim and June Young. Jim Young related that Martha was involved with a little girl with rabies who was in the process of taking the vaccine. It was a painful process, and there was some question as to whether it was necessary for her to take the vaccine, but better safe than sorry. The little girl died shortly after admission.

Young added, "This is a terrible disease, and we've had a number of cases here over the years. One patient bit one of our nurses several years ago. Fortunately, the vaccine was effective." Treating the little girl must have been an eye-opening experience for the 33-year-old doctor from Alabama, but the card doesn't say how Martha reacted to the situation.

Others filled in the gaps about Martha.

Martha—through the eyes of Susan Pirtle

Ronald and Susan Pirtle were appointed career missionaries by the Foreign Mission Board (now International Mission Board) in July 1973. They arrived in Yemen in May 1974. They first met Martha when she arrived in 1978. They had already heard about Martha from some of the others who knew her during the receptorship. They had been told she was different, doing things in her own way and in her own time.

"My first impressions were that I liked her," remembers Susan. "She was very friendly and always had a big smile on her face."

From the beginning she plunged into the work and into language study. As Susan got to know Martha she began to see her differentness.

"She had this focus totally on the Yemenis. She was so focused that she neglected her own self. Her house was a place to sleep—if she slept. . . . It sometimes seemed that she never slept or was ever at home. It seemed she was ALWAYS at the hospital. Many times she would be found sleeping in the chapel or on one of the gurneys.

"I am not sure when she ate. Maybe on the run or whenever she happened to be around where there was food."

Susan declares she's never known anyone like Martha. She was the most selfless person that she's ever known.

"Martha loved the Yemeni people with a passion. Everything she did was for them—and they knew it. Being an OB/GYN physician, she had the unique opportunity to help the ladies of Yemen that many did not. They all loved her. She even let her long-staying patients live in her home. They even became caretakers for Martha. They cooked for her and even kept house for her—all from a love for a woman who devoted all of her life for them."

When one of Susan's sons was a young teenager he told his mother that Martha was the closest person to Lottie Moon that he knew—and he knew a lot of missionaries.

Martha loved the children of the hospital compound. She was famous for bringing camels on the compound so that everyone could ride them. It was a big treat for all the children—adults, too!

"She would take our children with her on some of her outings. They especially liked going to see the baboons! In her relationships with our children you could see in Martha her childlike spirit—her joy in everything she did.

"Martha often ate with our family, and occasionally we ate with her in her home. Cooking was not one of her accomplishments, but we always had a wonderful time. The children always considered it a special treat to be invited to Martha's for supper. We always had mutton."

Susan says one of her most memorable experiences with Martha came when one of Susan's Yemeni friends had a baby.

"I had known Nafisa since she was 9 years old. She married when she was a teenager. As a child she was at my home almost every day, dirty and most unladylike. But she grew up into a beautiful young woman.

"Martha came to get me one afternoon. Nafisa was in labor with her first baby. Her mother could not be with her during the delivery and Nafisa wanted me to be with her. So I was able to be the 'grandmother' for the first baby of my little friend. During this delivery I was able to see Martha at work. She was so calm and reassuring to Nafisa. I really feel because of Martha's calm demeanor that Nafisa remained calm. I was amazed at how wonderfully Nafisa did during the delivery. To this day I have always felt honored to have been a part of this time in the life of my friends: Nafisa and Martha.

Martha was truly a biblical Martha—completely devoted to her Lord, always working, doing for others, never thinking of herself. But she was also Mary in her work, sitting at His feet."

Martha—through the eyes of Ron Pirtle

"It was so apparent how much Martha loved the Yemeni people. She was down at the hospital much more than she was ever at home. I would go down to the hospital to see an emergency patient when I was on call and there was Martha sitting and eating or just talking with the patients and our Yemeni hospital staff. This could happen in the middle of the night or on weekends—any time was the right time for Martha to be ministering.

"She rarely was at home. Much of the time she let one of her fistula patients live in her house because they had nowhere else to go—many of them came from far away. Their families shunned them because of the constant leakage of urine and the bad smell. Their treatment often required long stays and multiple surgeries. To free up an extra hospital bed for another patient, Martha invited them to live with her. I often wonder how many of these ladies came to know the Lord through Martha's ministry.

"She was always going to others' homes for a meal, a wedding, or a funeral. She loved being with the Yemeni people.

"Some of us loved the work, but Martha loved the people. I think she was like her Lord and heard Him say, "Well done, my good and faithful servant.""

Martha—through the eyes of the Pirtle children

Stephen, the first Pirtle son, at age 35, said, "I knew 'Aunt Martha' as we called her, since I was 9. She was like family to us. I remember excursions into Jibla and the surrounding villages with her. Soon-to-be mommies and children would always come out to meet Martha so that she could check them out to make sure they were OK. She loved what she did and you could tell it by her actions."

Marc, the second Pirtle son, had known Martha since he was 6½. At age 33 he said, "Samantha Koehn and I would go with Martha on her trips to the villages to vaccinate children. There would always be lots of children, all trying to see Martha. We had a great time on these trips, going out into the middle of nowhere.

"I loved her personality. There was no one else like her. She was the coolest person I knew. Samantha and I were 15 years old on these adventures."

Joel, the third son, knew Martha from the time he was 2 years old. At age 28 he said, "I have fond memories of riding camels and eating at Martha's house.

"Her house was always very cluttered, everything was everywhere. I later learned that she didn't throw anything away because someone might need it. She gave away most everything she had to those in need. She didn't hold on to anything for herself. Her things were always for others.

"Martha was different. She was more like a Yemeni than a Westerner. She had become completely acclimated to the culture. She knew the people, who they were, how they lived, what they needed. Therefore, she was able to share Christ in ways others could not."

Elizabeth Pirtle Baker, the only Pirtle daughter and the youngest child, was 18 months old when Martha came into her life. At age 25 she said, "A few days before my family and I left Yemen for good, I found a small treasure under my pillow. After waking from a night's sleep, I stretched my arms under my pillow and felt something cold brush against my hand. As I raised my pillow the morning sun shone on a green marble stone shaped into a heart. I searched around to find out who it was from. Not until the end of the day did I find out. A note was found tucked under my bed. It read:

Dear Liz,
Here is a small heart locket for you. Whenever you look at it may you remember Yemen and your family.
Love,
Aunt Martha

"I still have my heart treasure today, reminding me of my home in Yemen and my family, especially Aunt Martha, who always shared this great love to all the compound kids."

Susan ends these wonderful "looks" by saying, "It was very hard for us to express ourselves concerning someone we loved. I guess we are still not completely accepting that she has died. She was such an 'alive' person."

9
Memories from the 1980s

For most Americans, the end of the 1970s and the coming of the 1980s was marked by the Iran hostage crisis, the election of Ronald Reagan, and the transformation of baby boomers from idealist hippies into consumerist yuppies. The message everywhere was "Me first." Even a lot of Christians were influenced by the message, and started putting more money into large homes, large churches, large cars—well, just large everything!

Some people, though, were not influenced by the "me first" message. Martha was one of those. She believed in putting others first. That's not to say she was not affected by the people around her. Some of the most influential people in Martha's life were the nurses at Jibla Baptist Hospital. Leading the list is Australian contract nurse Ethne Stainer, who worked in Gaza before coming to Yemen. In fact, she was a contract nurse from 1959 until 1973. In 1973 something rare and wonderful happened. Ethne was appointed as a career Southern Baptist missionary. She served in that capacity until her retirement in 1992.

Her heart's desire was to retire in America where she had many friends. She tried for a year to obtain a visa, but to no avail. She went then to her home country of Australia.

Having served so long already in the Middle East, Ethne was equipped to be Martha's mentor during Martha's early years. They loved each other and prayed together often. She understood Martha. We'll understand her better by looking through the eyes of Ethne.

Martha—through the eyes of Ethne Stainer

"Martha was a good friend of mine during our years in Yemen. She was an excellent doctor, surgeon, and obstetrician. She worked hard and had a kind, loving, compassionate heart, with no thought for her own needs—such as food and sleep.

"Unfortunately, Martha was often misunderstood because she was an individual worker and really did not always work well with others. Time and hospital routines and schedules meant nothing to her.

"Her time was spent and her heart was given to the Yemeni people 100 percent. Her house was always open and full of Yemeni visitors when she was home. In later years after I left she moved out of the compound and lived in the village of Ibb among the Yemenis. Actually there were a number of others who also moved to the village as the staff numbers increased.

"Her early years in Yemen were devoted to the hospital where she worked tirelessly—sometimes almost around the clock. Later she began a very important and challenging role—traveling into the villages to immunize the children who did not have access to hospital care in those early years when there were not roads or transport.

"This ministry grew until she spent most of her time out in the Land Cruiser. She covered hundreds of miles over rough, almost impassible, roads over high mountains. Then after a long, tiring journey, she worked tirelessly, sometimes even sleeping in the village.

"Besides the vaccinating, she treated and cared for many people, mainly women and children. They all adored her and many owe their lives to her care and concern.

"I spent precious times of fellowship and prayer with Martha, went on village trips with her, and enjoyed hospitality and fun in some Jibla houses with her.

"Martha loved the MKs and would sometimes arrive on the compound with a camel for them—and also for other bigger children (not me!) to ride and enjoy. It was always a fun time.

"To get a true picture of Martha in Yemen, you would need to interview the Yemenis that accompanied her on those village trips and traveled with her to those far and often isolated places.

"Martha was a true child and follower of her heavenly Father and the Lord Jesus. And she was able to tell many of these dear people about His love for them. All she did she did in His name and the Yemeni people saw the real love of Jesus as she served among them.

"I guess it is all summed up by what they wrote on her tombstone: *She loved God.* And she did and that love flowed out to the dear people she was called to minister to.

"I believe that many years in the future Martha will be the one they all remember, because she truly identified with them in every aspect of their lives. I believe we will meet some of these dear people in heaven as a result of Martha's ministry in the beautiful country of Yemen."

Martha—through the eyes of Ruth Anne McConnell

Ruth Anne McConnell went as a journeyman nurse to Yemen in 1977. (A journeyman is a young person who spends two years as an international missions volunteer with the Southern Baptist International Mission Board.) She returned as a career missionary in 1980 and served until 1996. She knew Martha as a friend and as a longtime co-worker in Jibla Baptist Hospital.

So many of the things that Martha did were out in the villages, Ruth Anne says. She really was a legend and known to everyone. People far away from Jibla knew who Martha was and all could tell some story about how she had helped them.

"One of the things I've always remembered about Martha was her love for the MKs and her patience. One time she was having several of us to her home for dinner. She had a great big jigsaw puzzle almost finished and one of the little kids (2 or 3 years old at the most) thought it was pretty and in his excitement knocked all the pieces to the floor. Martha didn't lose it or even seem upset. She laughed, pushed the pieces aside, and went on with her party. She didn't seem upset at all.

"At Christmas, we often had an MK party. One of the treats Martha often provided was a camel for the kids to ride. (Everybody remembers the camel!) It was great fun when Santa came in on the camel with his bag of toys.

"Martha in the clinic was always a challenge. She kept her own schedule and never rushed. She had the skill of being totally involved with the person she was talking to and blocking out all the things going on around her. When the crowds were fussing at me, I didn't always see that as a positive, but the people she was with knew they had her full attention and she would do whatever she needed to do to get them the help they needed. She would take them to other cities and doctors if they didn't have transportation. She always had a full load of people waiting for her wherever she was going."

Ruth Anne was able to witness the way the people showed their love for Martha, in return for her love for them. Martha accepted their gifts and gestures with warmth and grace, even when the gifts were a little more down-to-earth than what Americans might expect.

"I'll never forget the time we had a shortage of imported (clean and frozen) chickens. Most of us were just doing without. One day a little man came in with a live chicken for Martha. I'm sure she took it and used it. I'm not real sure where the chicken went after the man went through the clinic looking for Martha!

"It's for sure, anything could happen when Martha was around! At least, that's the way I saw it."

10
A Family of Nurses

Robert and Bev Thomas, both nurses, arrived in Jibla in April 1981, but they first encountered Martha at Callaway Gardens, Georgia, during missionary orientation. Her entrance into their lives was classic Martha.

Martha—through the eyes of Bev Thomas

"I met Martha in the winter of 1981 at Callaway Gardens, Georgia. Bob and I were in the next to last orientation group that had field training at Callaway. We arrived on January 2 and it was a very cold winter. Bob and I had two little girls: Tracy, 2½ years old, and Ginny, 2 months old.

"It was very late one night, around midnight. I was lying on the couch trying to get Ginny asleep. There was a knock on our cabin door. I asked who was there and slowly cracked open the door.

"There stood a woman I had never seen before, suitcase in hand. 'Hi, I'm Martha,' she said and I knew immediately that it was Martha 'from Yemen.' Martha was scheduled to be a guest speaker to the orientation group that week. She had arrived a few days early and ended up on our porch at midnight. As far as I can remember, Martha stayed with us for several days.

"She spoke to the orientation group, but I must say that some were a little amused by her choice of clothing. She made no distinction between Yemen dress and American dress. Bob and I were into jogging at Callaway and nothing would do but that Martha get a bike and go with us. I will never forget her trying to ride a bike with flowing skirts and boots.

"Martha spent a lot of time with us and also with the Lindholms, Al and Edna, who were also going to Yemen. Also, there was a young Yemeni man in training at Fort Benning in Columbus, Georgia. He came to Callaway for some reason. I think it was an international weekend—and I remember Martha spent so much time with him and particularly enjoyed conversing with him in Arabic.

"Bob and I and the girls arrived in Jibla in April 1981. We studied Arabic for about six weeks and then worked in the hospital two weeks. This schedule went on for about 9 months. Those were very busy days at the hospital and nurses were in short supply. Bob was to work in the men's ward and I was trained by Ethne Stainer in midwifery and began working in the evenings on the women's ward and delivery room. Martha was a real specialist in this area.

"Ethne trained us nurses to do normal deliveries (and also not-so-normal ones) but she helped us know when to call for the help of a midwife or physician. I worked on and off in the delivery room for several years and called for Martha's help many times. She never belittled me or questioned my judgment. I always knew that she would come if I called for her. It would usually take her a while before she would finally make it, however.

"We had a particularly difficult time, all of us at Jibla, the Ramadan* after the Persian Gulf War of 1991. Staffing at the hospital was pitifully low because so many of the Filipino and Indian nurses left because of the possible danger. Bob scheduled three nurses to take care of the hospital during the morning shift. He and I took it on the evening shift. He took the men and children's wards and the outpatient clinic. I took the delivery room and women's ward. We had one nursing assistant each. It was an impossible task and we were all exhausted. Our children even got involved in helping out. Tracy was 11 and she worked in the pharmacy with Bernie and Annette Fairchild. Ginny was 9 and she helped me in the delivery room.

"There was one evening that was absolutely crazy. I had something like eight patients in the delivery room. I would deliver the baby and give him or her to Ginny and she would weigh it and get it swaddled up and all. After one birth she came to me as I was rushing around and said, 'Mom, I think there is something wrong with this baby's feet.' Sure enough, the baby had club feet. I sent Ginny for Martha and together they got the baby put into leg casts.

"Then there was an evening when one of the ladies needed a C-section. I asked Martha if Ginny could observe the procedure in the operating room. Martha was thrilled and used it as a teaching experience for a little 9-year-old girl. I will never forget Ginny dressed in scrubs bringing this little baby to the delivery room to be weighed. She was so excited. I know that those experiences had to play a part into why Ginny is a nurse today working with moms and babies.

"We had a tradition at Jibla in giving each child a birthday party. In the early days even the adults came to celebrate with cake and Kool-Aid and a small gift. The kids grew up feeling very special and loved by their 'aunts and uncles.' None was more loved than Aunt Martha. She always came up with the most unusual gifts. You never knew what to expect. Ginny was blessed on her tenth birthday with a falcon—dead and suspended on a hanger. The thing was huge! The bad part was when it started molting; there were feathers all over the hill behind our house. The falcon was disposed of quickly.

"In 1987 our kids came up with an idea to raise money to help fund our multipurpose building. Prior to this time, we had all our worship services in different homes, but the time had come when we had to have more room. The International Mission Board allowed us to build the building, but could not help with the funding. All of us on the compound plus private donations funded the building. Thanksgiving of 1987, the kids organized games, food, auctions—all sorts of things. The parents cooked all the food and then bought it all back! It was great fun. From 1988 through 2002, the money earned from the Autumn Fair went to the Lottie Moon offering.

"Martha's contribution every year was to schedule the Bedouins who lived in the *wadi* to come in with their camels. Martha paid the men and boys to bring the camels and give camel rides to all interested persons.

"A woman's conference was held for the ladies in the Middle East in October 2002 on Cyprus. Martha was there along with many of us from Yemen. We had a small choir and Martha and I sang in it. She looked so pretty. I like to remember her just like that."

Martha—through the eyes of Bob Thomas

"Remembering Martha brings back several feelings: humorous, serious, dedication, and even disillusion. One thing I remember about Martha which frustrated many of us was her 'clock.' Martha didn't have one. That would mean that if you made an appointment with her, you would see her that day, unless, of course, it was a real emergency.

"Now for a few of the other feelings: humorous (unless it might be at your expense): Martha had a penchant for picking up stray animals. One of her particular favorites were monkeys. When we first arrived in Yemen, the upper hills were full of wild monkeys. The Yemeni kids would go out, capture the monkeys, tie them up, and generally mistreat them. On several occasions, Martha purchased the monkey. I think in one sense this was to give money to the impoverished kid, but also so the monkey would not suffer. One such monkey she brought back to the compound and tied to the tree near her house.

"I was the community gardener. I remember putting out tomato plants during the time Martha had her monkey. Now these tomato plants weren't the variety you could go to the local Wal-Mart or Home Depot and buy. These were tomato plants that had been nurtured from seeds (seeds purchased in my home state of Mississippi, real homegrown tomatoes). I had planted them several weeks earlier, and had just transplanted about 15 plants a few days before.

"To make a long story short, Martha's monkey broke free and started running around the compound. The compound is 21 acres on which the hospital and houses are located. The monkey targeted my tomato plants. It systematically went from one tomato plant to the next, pulling them up, and examining them as if to say, 'Ah, this is an interesting specimen.'

"All 15 plants were lost. For years, when we looked back on this episode, we laughed, although I must admit that most of the folks laughed more than I did. Martha could be compared to Dennis the Menace!

"Another feeling: serious. Martha loved the Lord. I remember on several occasions making rounds with Martha in the hospital. Even before the days when chronological Bible storying was popular, Martha could take life events and use Bible stories to illustrate her point.

"One of the leading causes of infant death in Yemen and the unreached world is pneumonia. In many instances this is brought about by diarrhea, which dehydrates the baby and causes it's health to go down quickly. A major cause of diarrhea comes from ill-prepared formulas for infants, or even worse, bottles that sit around for a day or two and then the mother gives the bottle of spoiled milk to the baby.

"I would like to reiterate that this was usually based on ignorance of the mother about spoilage and the fact that most were so poor that they didn't want to waste anything. One of Martha's teaching tools while on rounds was to always check the baby's bottles. She would do this by removing the cap and smelling the formula. If it was sour, she would always hand it back to the mother and ask her to drink it. At one whiff the mother would generally refuse. Martha would then reply, 'And you think the baby is OK with this?'

"Martha was a good teacher.

"Another feeling: caring. Martha was a true advocate for the peoples of Yemen. She would stand up for them to the end. Although it is true that we would like to do whatever we could for the peoples of Yemen, at times that just wasn't possible. Anyone seeking to meet every need presented them during even one day at Jibla Baptist Hospital would be crazy by the end of the day.

"One such point was in the treatment of burn cases. As a hospital committee, we met on several occasions to discuss treatment options for special cases such as burns. Burn cases required intensive, intensive (note the emphasis) nursing care and taxed our staff tremendously. Imagine dressing burns daily as patients scream in pain. Imagine the financial resources to treat burns. Mission hospitals do not have huge resources to spend on just one classification of patient. Yet, we tried to do everything we could possibly do to help the patients.

"As a hospital, our overriding policy was that no one would be turned away, especially if they were in serious condition. And, as a committee, we had agreed that we would not send patients off until they were stable enough to travel. But we also decided that seven burn patients at one time was all that we could accept. We were, by the way, the premier burn care center in the country with a fairly high survival rate if we could get the burns past the first 72 to 96 hours. Martha fought this policy of accepting no more than seven burn patients, knowing that the patients had come to Jibla for help and that they would probably receive lesser care at any other hospital. This was a true dilemma for us and Martha was always the advocate for the Yemeni point of view.

"Martha contributed (no matter what): One remembrance of Martha was at a New Year's Eve party. She had signed up to bring dessert. Martha was notorious for starting something and doing several things in between, in an effort to accomplish several tasks within a given time frame. When Martha arrived at the party, she came with her two cakes, both charred black. She had put them in the oven and then went about several other tasks. She decided to come back and get them eight hours later. She brought them to the party to show that she had truly meant to honor her commitment!

"I've tried to show that Martha was a real person. She had faults, just as we do. She wasn't perfect. But her love for the Yemeni people was only surpassed by her love for God. Martha will truly be missed by the peoples of Yemen. She had a relationship with many of them that we only dream of having. She gave herself totally to them.

"According to reports taken from the one who shot her, it was this fact that led to

Martha's death. The wife of the man who shot her reported that her experience with Martha during a visit to the outpatient clinic was so powerful and full of love, that the man was prompted to 'do something about that Christian love that had such a power!' Oh, that we all could demonstrate Christ's love to others in such a manner."

---

*Ramadan is the monthlong fast which devout Muslims undergo each year. They fast through the day and break their fast only at night. As one of the five pillars of Islamic faith, Ramadan is a time of great significance.

11
A Tennessee Nurse Looks at Martha

Leslie Durham from Tennessee first went to Yemen as a journeyman in 1985. She returned as a career missionary in 1993 and stayed through 2000.

Martha—through the eyes of Leslie Durham

Leslie remembers that she met the 40-year-old Martha in 1985. They had just arrived at the gate of Jibla Baptist Hospital from Sana'a, the capital, after the long flights to reach Yemen. The gate was surrounded by men in head scarves and skirts.

"Martha came out to open the gate for us. There was a ladder that went from the back of the Land Cruiser to the roof rack. Martha climbed onto that ladder like a Yemeni man and hung on as we drove up the hill to the houses. Having just arrived in the country I didn't realize that women did that sort of thing. I soon found out that women didn't, just Martha.

"That was when I first learned that Martha sang to the beat of a different drummer, so to speak.

"It was also the first time I, in my young nursing career, met a physician who preferred to be called by her first name and liked to socialize with nurses. We became friends. We didn't agree on several things. We worked a lot together. There were certainly many times I didn't understand Martha at all, and probably she had the same feeling about me. But I am proud to have known her and call her my friend.

"Martha was the Goodwill Queen. I doubt that she ever bought any piece of clothing new. Maybe she bought new shoes; in fact, I think she did. But clothes were NEVER new. Every furlough she came back with all kinds of outfits from church basements, Goodwill, and consignment stores. But the thing that amazed me was that she always looked good and neat. Everything matched and she carried herself like a finishing school graduate with perfect posture and never looked rumpled. She never even looked rumpled after having slept in her clothes all day or for several days. The latter is something she made a habit of doing. But she always had this air of someone who could be sitting with ankles crossed for hours and never looked bored or tired or strained.

"She was also one who truly didn't worry about the next meal or what she would wear or where she would get her next bath. She practiced what Jesus instructed the disciples to do, not to carry extra clothes or packs.

"Martha treated every person she met as though he or she were the most interesting person she'd ever met. No matter what they did or where they came from or what they talked about, she seemed to find it very interesting. After a conversation with her on the first meeting, I (and others) felt like I was so interesting or smart or insightful. She was great with names too. Never seemed to forget a face.

"There is no doubt that Martha was eccentric, sometimes really eccentric. I have to say that I rarely understood her—I mean how she thought. But somehow she seemed to be patient even if it took her forever to get her ideas and thoughts across.

"It was really neat to me the way that Martha got on with her parents. They just seemed to be good friends. They went places together. And they were close. She was especially close to her father.

"I also realized that she was very modest and humble. Her father had received a degree (it may have been a master's in public health, I am not sure) from some Ivy League medical school like Harvard or Yale. And Martha just mentioned that she spent some years growing up in New Haven or Boston. (Author's note: It was Harvard, a master's in public health.)

"She was always late, sometimes hours, for an appointment. She was even later if it was social. Once we had a surprise birthday party for her and all the missionaries had agreed to dress Yemeni style. She was hours and hours late (about two hours) busy with some emergency in the hospital. And the ladies were boiling in their Yemeni dress waiting for Martha.

"She was notorious for taking charts and x-rays with her on trips out of the hospital. She would have bags full of charts and x-rays that were all scratched up right up until the time the plane was leaving to take her to the USA for furlough.

"She was an amazing driver. I mean I have rarely seen or ridden with such a driver. She learned (I think but am not sure) from Mohammed Amin, her Yemeni brother. He was an excellent driver. Martha could take any turn with any load and go in reverse. She could whip in and out of four-wheel drive. She loved to take "new to the country" foreigners on *wadi* (creek) rides and usually some sort of stalling incident or car repair resulted. And they got to get one-on-one Yemeni interaction. I just know—deep down—Martha either orchestrated or prayed for these things to happen. But she was probably the best driver I have ever met. I'd match her with any over-the-road truck driver in the USA.

"Once when we were going to a fancy expat (short for expatriate) ladies luncheon at a five-star hotel in the capital city, she had a turtle with her in the car. She loved to pick up animals on the road, and she gave them away or she doctored them up. She found this turtle and wanted to take it to one of the missionary families in the capital. Well, we were late and had to go straight to the restaurant. I thought she'd leave the turtle in the car. But no, she brought the turtle in his box and set it beside her on the floor.

"We were eating with embassy and oil company ladies. Of course, Martha wasn't intimidated by anyone. She treated everyone the same, really and truly. And she just talked with these ladies, like it was not unusual to bring a turtle to a five-star hotel luncheon. Pretty soon she had them all looking at her turtle and some of them offered her lettuce from their salad to feed the turtle. The Indian (Hindi vegetarian) servers were soon bringing her food for the turtle. I realized I was the only one who was embarrassed. Martha thought nothing of it. I looked at them and thought, 'Now, what is wrong with this picture?'

"Martha could sit for hours in a squatting position and be laughing and talking and gracious. She was the best guest you could hope to have. She ate anything and talked to everyone.

"It goes without saying that she was great with the language. She used the colloquialisms and slang. She was Yemeni except for her white skin—and she didn't wear a veil. And I have to say I never saw her in Yemeni baltho or sharshiff. She was covered from neck to ankles. And she wore glasses. Not many Yemeni ladies wore glasses.

"I also think she dreamed and thought in Arabic. She couldn't have a complete conversation in English. She often used a Yemeni word because she couldn't think of the English."

Leslie, like many others, noticed the relationship Martha had with her patients, especially the young mothers with fistulas. She recognized that they tried with their actions to show their love and gratitude to the doctor who had come to Yemen "for them."

Leslie recalled, "Martha would have probably never eaten or had clean clothes if not for the 'fistula ladies.' Since Martha did the surgical fistula repair of these women, who were outcasts, they showered her with love and affection. It is basically a condition where the bladder gets a hole (tires are tubeless now, but they used to have inner tubes. If a hole came in the inner tube, it had to be patched). If a hole comes in a person's bladder, she would constantly leak urine. It is usually the result of prolonged labor when the baby is too big for the mother or other complications like that. These women leak urine all the time, they cannot control it. Surgery is hard and often takes several months, even years, and often does not work. When you kiss the hands of these women in greeting, the Yemeni custom, you smell and taste urine.

"Martha would adopt these women, keep them at her house. They cooked and cleaned for her. They became mothers to her. And they were so much fun, cooking and cleaning and enjoying living on the compound.

"These women were social outcasts because they were unclean according to the culture and they often were shunned by families. There are several ladies like this who live and work at Jibla Baptist Hospital and have remarried and had more children. It is neat to see how Martha mentored them.

"Martha would frequently take in strays— people or animals. She also had eccentric characters as patients. She had mentally ill people. There was Saleh, who had chronic mental problems, I think. I also think he was treated badly by family. He walked everywhere. Martha took him in. I'm not sure where he lived but he came to the hospital all the time. He had this high squeaky voice and talked on only one volume: loud! And he adored her.

"Then there was the lady who was older and outcast and Martha got her adopted by a local Yemeni family and she had a room in their house. It was so neat to see her mentor that type of attitude in her local friends. Though many Yemenis didn't need prompting on that.

"Somehow people knew the place to come if you needed any type of help was to Martha. She helped all kinds of unwed mothers (capital punishment here) get their babies away from families. She could figure out some kind of angle that worked within the cultural guidelines and kept most at peace. She really was great at working within the Yemeni guidelines. She didn't come in and try to make things work the American way like a lot of us did. It was amazing how God used her that way.

"I don't think I ever met a child Martha didn't like and who didn't like Martha. She had a way with children. They trusted her. Actually, thinking about it, she could charm everyone from the most stoic, conservative Yemeni man to the most terrified Yemeni lady. She really could get them to listen to her.

"Martha had a sixth sense about needs in the hospital, whether it was a 'political' situation or a medical emergency. Before you knew it, Martha was there. She would just appear, whether she was on call or not. Usually the newer doctors wanted her back-up for the delivery room anyway. If you had a bleeding lady or a baby with an overdose or a terrible car accident victim, Martha would turn up. It was such a relief because Martha always had an answer culturally, spiritually, and medically. It was such a relief, especially when I as the nurse needed help. Martha was a rock to lean on.

"I can't imagine Yemen without Martha. And I am sure there are Yemenis who feel the same. She gave everything she had. She literally gave away the last rial (Yemeni money) she had and the shirt off her back.

"But she was a maverick, a free spirit, an individual who could have survived out in the village without any other American. She really was the twentieth-century Lottie Moon."

12
A Yemeni
Missionary
Matriarch

Roberta Kells Dorr is truly a matriarch of the Yemeni team. She went to Yemen with her husband, David Dorr, and their three children in 1969. She met Martha, however, when she was home on furlough (now stateside assignment) at a medical meeting. Martha had come with her father. She looked very young and Roberta assumed she was a college student. She came over to Roberta and began asking her questions about Yemen—especially about the women and children.

Since Roberta loves to talk about the women and children, she told her many things. The more she talked, the more interested Martha became.

"What about them medically? What are their needs?" Martha asked. Something about the way she asked had a sense of urgency. Roberta hesitated. It was such an adult question.

"Why are you interested?" she finally asked.

Martha responded by telling her that she was in her residency in obstetrics and that she was considering places in the world where they might need an obstetrician, especially a woman obstetrician. Martha added, "I want to go some place where I am really needed."

Roberta was surprised that such a young, pretty girl was an obstetrician and was looking for a place of real need. Then she thought of the multiple problems of young girls and women in Yemen. Could she possibly be ready for such a challenge?

The needs were unique—even frightening. "It was a place where very young girls could be married to mature men and often became pregnant before their immature bodies were ready. The pain and suffering this caused was almost impossible for the average person to imagine. The young girl could spend hours in painful delivery with only ignorant midwives to attend them and the result was almost always a dead baby and the young mother hopelessly torn beyond repair."

Roberta hesitated—not wanting to tell such a shocking story to someone so eager to face difficulty. But Martha sensed her reluctance and urged her to tell why she was holding back.

"It's not something we talk about very often," Roberta explained. "It's hard for Americans to understand."

Martha explained that she wanted to know; she needed to know.

So, as briefly as she could, Roberta explained, watching to see how Martha reacted. She became very still and she didn't speak for a moment. Then she asked, "What happens to the women then?"

"They are divorced and sent home to their parents."

"And?" Martha probed.

"They spend the rest of their lives as outcasts in some back room. They have no control of their bowels and the odor is terrible."

"Thank you, thank you," she said finally. "That is what I wanted to know."

The next session of the medical meeting was announced, so the encounter ended. She felt sad and guilty that she had explained so much. "Well, that is one person who will never come to Yemen."

Roberta continues by saying her family was back in Yemen before she heard that Martha had been appointed and would be arriving soon. Martha had meant what she said. She wanted to go where she was most needed!

She blossomed and bloomed in Yemen, the hard place, Roberta claims. She loved the mountains, the flowers, the unusual birds, but she spent her time with the women and children. She became a part of their lives.

The time came when the Dorrs had to leave Yemen and their hearts were torn wondering if they would ever again see these people that they loved.

"But Martha wrote and told me about my friends and she told David what was happening in the hospital."

Then something unexpected happened that brought Roberta back to Yemen. Two of her novels had been published and she was working on a third, telling the story of the Queen of Sheba's visit to Solomon. She had collected many stories and legends of the queen in both Yemen and Ethiopia, yet she had never been able to visit the site of the queen's palace in Marib.

Her son John was doing relief work in Yemen and wrote to say if she could come, he had a car available and could drive her to Marib. He also said the museum in Sana'a had been opened with many new finds and it would be a great help. Roberta wrote to Martha with the news and Martha wrote back insisting that John and she must make the long drive down to Jibla.

Everything worked out as planned. When Roberta arrived at the hospital, Martha was working, but she insisted that she go on to her house and she would follow shortly. She added that she had a patient and her family in her living room. "Just relax and enjoy them until I come."

When Roberta arrived at Martha's small house, she found a young girl on her sofa bed in the living room and five other older women sitting around. One had a small stove and was cooking something right in the middle of the floor. "Ahlan, ahlan," they said as another woman hustled a chicken off a chair and motioned for Roberta to sit down. She did and then looked around. It was July but Martha's small Christmas tree was still sitting on the coffee table. There were bedrolls in one corner and she realized that all these women were spending the night here also.

The women talked all at once telling Roberta about the young girl in the bed and how Martha had not only operated on her but had brought her to her house when she could no longer stay in the hospital. "Martha never sleeps," they said. "She always working, working for people who are sick."

When Martha finally arrived, she explained that she hadn't had time to take down the Christmas tree; and besides, the women loved the tree. The chickens were the food the women brought from their village.

"I don't mind," Martha said. "The important thing is that Assia nearly died and now she is almost well enough to go home." Martha hugged Assia as she asked her questions in Arabic. After each answer, Martha smiled and looked around at the women who nodded and smiled their delight.

Roberta saw Martha one more time, at her home in Montgomery during Martha's furlough. She had called asking to buy 50 of Roberta's books. Roberta was overwhelmed.

"You won't have space to pack that many."

"I'll get them in," she said. "There are many people who read English now and they have nothing interesting to read. They love your novel about the Queen of Sheba. You probably don't know that Mohamed Gorbani's son used your book to write a paper that got him a Fulbright scholarship."

Of course, Roberta hadn't known that and was astonished.

When Roberta's son Philip packed up the books and they were ready to send them, he said, "For what it will cost and the time it will take, we can drive to Montgomery with them and see Martha." So they loaded them into the car and headed south.

Martha was delighted to see them and they were glad to see her father and mother again and meet Joanna, whom they had not met before. They sat around the kitchen table and drank coffee and shared happy memories of Yemen. On hearing that her mother was suffering from a terminal case of cancer, they were immediately aware of how difficult this leaving was going to be for Martha. When she returned again, her mother would not be there to meet her.

Roberta marveled at Dorothy's quiet assurance that, of course, Martha must go. How hard this was for her father they could also understand. What an amazing family Martha had. None of them thought selfishly of what they wanted.

"Martha's life is there in Yemen and that is where she belongs," her mother said.

It seemed just a short time later that Roberta received the news that Martha, along with Bill Koehn and Kathleen Gariety, had been killed. She later learned that a man by the name of Abed Abdul Razzak Kamel had been the gunman.

"It was ironic that he had first come to the hospital with his wife to get Martha's help. He said his wife had difficulty in getting pregnant and Martha was trying to help. Martha was well aware that if the woman could not produce a child, the man would divorce her.

"When questioned, Kamel said that he was also angry because he had heard that all of Jibla was being influenced to become Christians. Kamel was not from Jibla and he later added that he was convinced that Martha and other people at the hospital were actually making sure that women would not have Muslim babies.

"When the people of Jibla heard of the tragedy at the hospital, they were devastated. They wept and ran screaming the unthinkable news through the village. They shared stories of the goodness and compassion of those who had been shot. Then, when the funerals were held, they gathered in long lines in every direction out from the hospital. They could not believe that such a disaster could come to their village in one day and at the hand of a stranger.

"Even in death Martha would not be returning home but would be buried on the hillside above the hospital. There are no Christian cemeteries in Yemen and Christians cannot be buried in Muslim cemeteries. Strangely enough, this hillside where the hospital and all our houses were built was once a Muslim cemetery. It was very old and most of the graves were no longer marked, so the people of the village of Jibla had agreed for the hospital to be built there. That's how it happened that just outside the back door of the house we lived in was an ancient stone half buried in the grass with the words faintly visible, *Allah Akbar,* or 'God is great.'

"How strange," Roberta thought, "that on this hillside where Martha lies buried, another revelation of God will stand as a reminder to everyone who passes by, for Martha came to this place with the awesome news that 'God is love.' Martha would have liked that."

Martha as a candle lighter in a family friend's wedding.

Martha at ten years old

Martha, *third from left*, was an active GA at Dalraida Baptist Church. Her mother, Dorothy, is standing behind her.

1963 high school graduation

Martha visiting friends in Germany

In 1966, Martha served as a summer missionary to Rochester Baptist
Church in New York.

1976 International Mission Board appointment

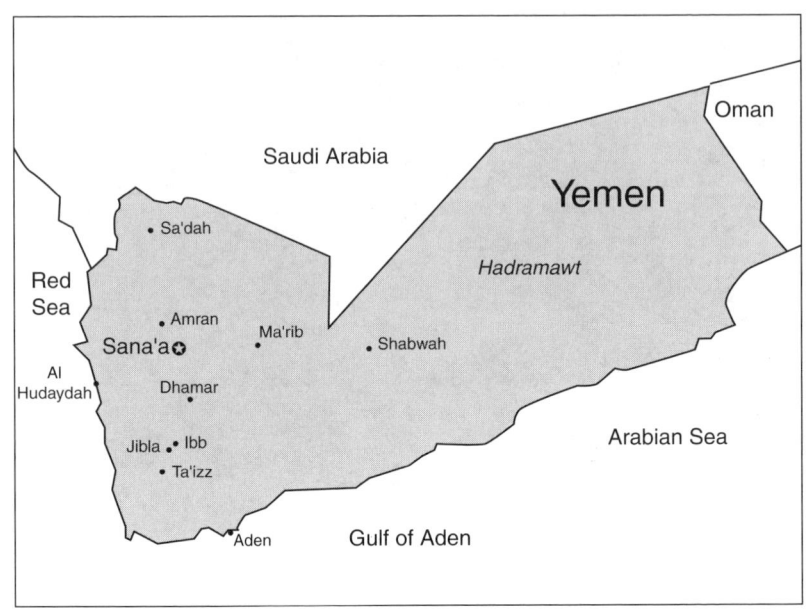

Yemen

Jibla, Yemen

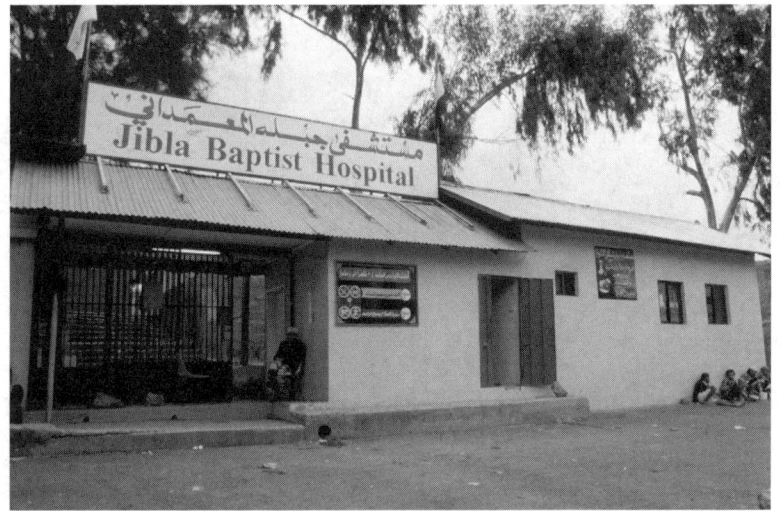

Jibla Baptist Hospital

Aerial view of Jibla Baptist Hospital compound

Aerial view of medical staff housing

Part of a Yemeni man's traditional dress, curved daggers, known as *jamibyas*, serves as status symbols.

Martha at work in Yemen with Bill Koehn and Yemeni co-worker

Martha and one of her pets, a ball python

Martha and more of her pets, geckos

Martha loved to hire camels for the children to ride.

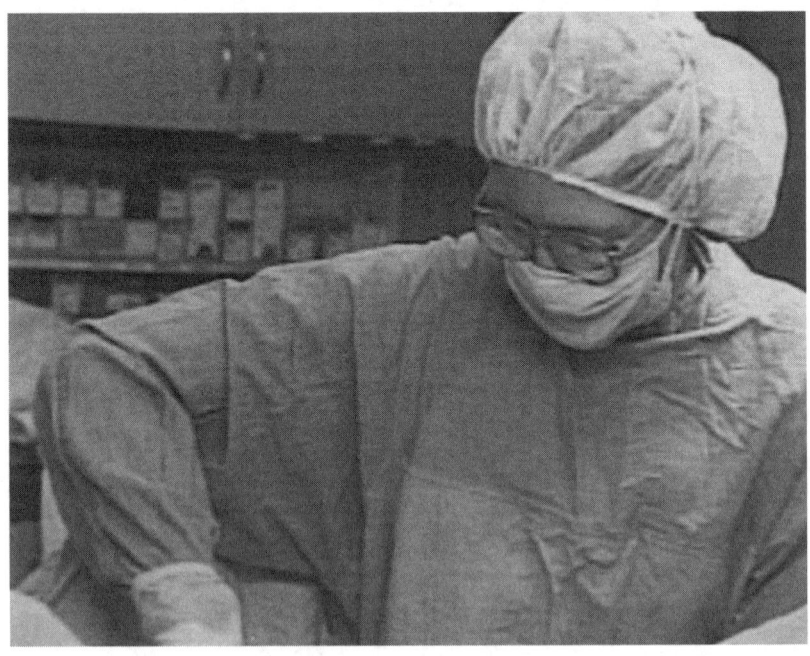

Martha performing surgery

Martha outside her home in Jibla

Martha loved to connect with the Yemeni children.

Martha distributing immunizations from the back of her truck

Martha and hospital co-worker examining an artisan's work

Martha sitting at her desk working on paperwork

Martha, Dorothy Myers, and Bill Wagner sharing a picnic breakfast on the outskirts of Jibla

A glimpse of God's glory over a Yemeni city

Dr. Martha Myers (1945–2002)

13
Celebrating Contract Workers

Jibla Baptist Hospital could not have functioned without the superlative contract nurses and doctors. One of the best of these was Cynthia Lagadan, a Filipino nurse who worked with Martha for 13 years. She saw Martha up close and personal.

Martha—through the eyes of Cynthia Lagadan
"The hospital was her house. She could lay down her head anywhere space was available: the library, EPI (Expanded Program of Immunization) office. One night shift while doing nursing rounds, I saw someone lying on the stretcher along the hallway. I thought he was a Yemeni patient's watcher and out of curiosity and concern I went close to see and found out that she is Doctura Martha covered nicely with a hospital blanket. I can only recognize her because she didn't cover her face. So many times she would just curl up on empty patient beds or even sleep on the floor with the Yemeni lady watchers when the hospital was full."

At midnight, the ward was full and so busy.

Nurses would run here and there attending to the never-ending needs and demands of patients. As Cynthia was struggling to insert an IV in a burn patient, suddenly someone stood beside her and patted her back. It was Martha. All she said was, "Cynthia, relax. God is in charge. I will be in Mr. Bill's office if you need me. Please wake me up at 5:30 A.M. I need to bring Fatma to the village."

Cynthia recalled, "Because the hospital was her house it was advantageous in some ways because we could call her, especially for difficult delivery assistance. Pulling babies from their dugouts was not fun and emotionally draining sometimes. Delivery room experiences can be very hard—like draining a hydrocephalic head or turning a breech position."

Martha possessed a huge, compassionate heart. Even when she was not on call, she would appear to help—even if not asked.

When Martha was still living in the compound, she used to accommodate in her house some discharged patients who lived far away from the hospital. The patient slept on her bed and Martha slept on her couch. Sometimes Martha would call Cynthia by phone asking for a favor—to bring sugar and tea to her house for a patient staying there.

"Martha had a lot of Christian books. She was very generous in lending her books to the nurses. One book's title was *Peacemaker.* She gave it to this operating room nurse to read. When the nurse returned the book, she told her to pass it on to others and to tell them to have peace. This was at the time that the hospital was very near to sinking down.

"In one of her books that I read, she had written by hand in Arabic an Arab proverb, "One hand cannot clap alone."

Australians Ken Kclezy and his wife, Gwen, were contract workers until the middle of June 2004. They are now back at home. Ken Kclezy wrote a tribute to Martha.

Martha—through the eyes of Ken Kclezy

"Gwen and I describe Jibla as a colony of heaven and value our time there as the most wonderful in our lives. We made lifelong friends and would like to go back. Some are still there.

"One of our best friends was Martha Myers. If ever we knew someone who fit Paul's ideal single person, totally devoted to doing the Lord's will, it was Martha. I doubt that she could have functioned as she did if she had responsibility for a husband and family.

"First, she had no conception of time, but a very good perception of eternity. This allowed her to devote whatever time was needed to the task at hand. No outpatient ever got short shrift because there was a long line of patients still waiting. This focus on each person coming to her clinic so impressed the wife of the man who eventually murdered her that she said to her husband on the way home that no Muslim doctor had ever treated her so kindly as Martha did. (She had had a bad experience. We know many excellent, courteous, and thoughtful Muslim doctors.) It was this incident that made him decide to kill Martha.

"All of this meant that Martha's clinics often ran overtime, which was of some inconvenience to management, but it rightly endeared her to thousands of Yemenis. When she was on a long leave (furlough [stateside assignment]) in 2001, a soldier at a checkpoint two hours north of Jibla asked us, "When is Dr. Martha coming back?" Others had similar experiences.

"It often happened that Martha's working day remained unfinished when others were on their way to bed. Gwen and I are late birds, and our front door was habitually open until well after 10:00 P.M., so Martha often dropped in to talk about the day. This could lead in all sorts of directions, and we soon knew that she had up-to-date knowledge of much behind-the-scenes activity, good or bad, in Ibb. I think she was the first of us to know about various Ibb officials' plans to dispose of Jibla Baptist Hospital after the Southern Baptists walked away. She knew a great number of Yemeni believers and was responsible under God for the conversion of many of them, and discipled them.

"We often asked her if she had eaten, and the usual answer, even at 10:30 P.M., was no." Gwen always had food about, and could flick on the microwave if necessary. Martha had many such meals with us.

"Second, if it is ever proper to describe someone as generous to a fault, it was Martha. If she saw someone in need, she had no hesitation in giving money. Others sometimes saw her as being taken in, but she knew very well that there is nothing in Scripture warning us to be overcareful not to be duped. (I have been constantly amazed, all my life, at the reasons Christians sometimes give for not giving money when there is an obvious need. No doubt there are 'rice Christians' out there, but most people are unscripturally frightened of giving them a red cent. I believe that all too often this leads to habitual holy parsimony that is quite disgraceful.)

"So this meant that Martha gave *liberally* (a word we do find in the Bible) to a degree that would scarcely have been possible had she not been single. She spent her money on others in all sorts of ways. There was the case of Leila, a Christian girl, in need of a kidney transplant abroad. What Martha simply did not have to give herself, she sought from others, and the transplant was done.

"She bought herself a TV and she turned up at our house with it saying she had nowhere to put it, so would we mind it for her? Nothing was said, but I think she felt that we were in need of this particular creature comfort. We enjoyed it for a couple of years, and when we went back to Jibla a little over a year ago, there it was again, in our next house.

"Gwen was in a party, including Martha, that visited the Hadhramaut* in late 1999. Martha's photos were much better than Gwen's so she turned up at our house with a duplicate set of them for us. A small thing, perhaps, but now a treasured reminder of her, of great sentimental value."

*Hadhramaut is a large territory of Yemen, and an important religious center. It is famous for its ancient mud skyscrapers, wadi, fort, beaches, sultan's palace, and museum.

14
The Edwards Family

Stephen and Kandi Edwards and their three little girls arrived in Yemen in 1993. The girls grew up loving their Aunt Martha. Kathleen was 2 years old when she met Martha, Kristina was 4 years old, and Kimberly was 6 years old.

Martha—through the eyes of Kathleen Edwards

"One of the things I remember most about Aunt Martha is that she always seemed to have animals. One day she came and showed me two iguana-type animals. They were scratched and looked rather bedraggled. She told us to rub them from head to tail and they wouldn't hurt you. If you rubbed them from tail to head, their scales would cut you. She stayed about 5 minutes and then she went visiting to show the animals to other kids.

"Whenever she had an animal, it was usually from a Yemeni family that wasn't caring for it well or it was hurt. It was like, if God created it, then it was important.

"Aunt Martha always wanted to help. When she shared God's love with someone, it was almost always returned. I remember one day she went visiting with my mom, my sisters, and me. We went to a Yemeni lady's house, and Aunt Martha talked with her the whole time. (I don't know what they said exactly because they were speaking in Arabic.) I just remember that the lady and Aunt Martha laughed a lot. I thought it was strange because that lady hadn't ever laughed in all the times our family had visited with her.

"When we left, she hugged Aunt Martha a long time, then she cried when Aunt Martha left with us. Everywhere Aunt Martha went, it was like she gave all the love she could to anybody who would take it—even when they wouldn't take it. She was always loving and working for the people."

Martha—through the eyes of Kristina Edwards

"She and my mother used to go to the women's section of the prison to visit. One time my sisters and I went with them. We watched as she passed out little trinkets, jewelry, and blankets that her Yemeni friends had made. She had some necklaces that she bought from one Yemeni friend, which she gave to the ladies in the prison. (By the way, she gave my sisters and me each a necklace, and we wore them to her memorial service.) Then she talked with the prisoners who had stolen, killed, and committed other crimes, women she had befriended. Some of them had small children and babies who lived there in the prison with their mothers, as they had nowhere else to go. Aunt Martha examined them and carefully administered whatever medicine they needed, and then gave them small toys. It was obvious that she loved them, and they loved her right back.

"We visited long into the afternoon, and we sang a song or two as well. When we left, some of the women cried because they had enjoyed visiting with Aunt Martha so much. I think they wanted her to stay forever. I feel that way about her too."

Martha—through the eyes of Kimberly Edwards

"I was scared when my parents told me that Dr. Martha was coming to look at us. I hated doctors. The past four or five visits to the doctor in the States had resulted in shots, and lots of them. Naturally, being only 6 years old and having spent less than a week in a strange, new country sick as a dog from jet lag and a 14-hour flight in the smoking section of a Jordanian plane, I was nervous.

"When the doctor came into the room where my sisters and I were lying on our couches, I thought we were done for. She looked tall and had a scarf wrapped around her hair and a pouch fastened around her waist. She looked nice, but I knew from experience that looks were deceiving, especially when it came to doctors. I prepared myself for the worst. Then she stretched her hand out and laid it on my forehead. To my surprise, it was soft and cool and so was her voice. I don't remember what she said, but I remember her smooth and gentle voice. She moved to my sisters and felt their foreheads too. Then she was gone. I was quite taken aback . . . this doctor was different. She was our new Aunt Martha.

"I didn't get to see Aunt Martha too much, but when I did, she always had a story to tell or some strange animal in her arms. She knew everyone and everyone knew her. It was through her that my mom, my sisters, and I got to go and visit the ladies in the prison. That was an experience I will never forget. The ladies flocked around Aunt Martha, telling her which beads they wanted and describing to her all their problems.

"Their children loved her too. Her arrival meant a toy to play with or a pair of shoes. Aunt Martha was the source of happiness for the ladies in the prison. It was she who provided them something to do—making jewelry. It was also she who provided them and their children with medicine so that some might live to see the day of their release. Aunt Martha was their light in those dark prison rooms and that light gave them hope.

"The light of her life gave me hope too. I miss her light. I miss her hands, her voice, and her face. But I take courage in the fact that because she showed her light wherever she went and in whatever she did, I won't be the only one to see her face again."

Martha—through the eyes of Kandi Edwards

"I must confess it has been hard to put Martha down on paper. She was always so much bigger than this life . . . no matter where God had her planted. As so many others, I loved her dearly and still easily grieve her passing. She was not perfect and would not want attention drawn to her unless it stood in the shadow of our Savior's light. A good thing, because to truly understand Martha means you have to understand the One Who called her, kept her, and guided her hands.

"Someone from the International Mission Board said they wanted 'a story' about Martha at her memorial service. While I gave them their 'story' . . . I also reminded them that her story found its beginning and end in serving her King. Martha would not want the spotlight on herself but on Jesus and what He is doing in the precious country of Yemen.

"Ironic that now the three people the International Mission Board wants to tell stories about from Yemen were three that found their earthly home could be nowhere outside of Yemen and were dedicated to the Yemenis and the ministry of the hospital. They were grieving the loss of the hospital prior to the Lord calling them home. What a special God-thing that they did not have to see the day when the doors of the hospital were closed! God worked as only He could and I realize all those hours that we spent trying to convince the International Mission Board of the need for the hospital were marked with His exclamation point . . . the lives of three who loved and served Him to their last days. To God be the glory!

"Every newcomer to our international community wanted to go out with 'Dohkturah Martha.' She was known throughout Yemen. I never visited in a Yemeni home but what some family member in that home had encountered our Martha. The stories they shared ranged from Martha preventing a woman from having a nervous breakdown when the husband took another wife, to a young man with burns on his face and hands stating he owed each breath to her. The Lord used her dedication to Him to help save many Yemeni lives on this earth and for eternity. Her life's impact as a doctor, sister, friend, mentor, and Christ follower were easily noted in Yemen. Martha had become such a part of the Yemenis' lives and they such a part of her life that she was at home in any home and they claimed her as their own. The stories I would love to tell about Martha would endanger lives because Martha was involved with people. Names and places come to mind when I think of Martha. She was 'networking' long before it became a buzzword.

"Martha had learned to be content. She had that deep abiding faith in her Lord that allowed her to rest in His sovereignty. Things happened for a reason and she looked at everything she was given as potentially something she would need to give away. Martha could make treasure for someone out of our trash. I never thought of her as being rich, but she believed she had been given much, and felt much was required for her to return to those in need. Whatever she received in material wealth was given to someone she knew who needed it more. She was a catalyst.

"While Martha did not require much from life, she was a major contributor to our international family life in Jibla. To her nieces and nephews on the compound, Aunt Martha was simply awesome! People would bring injured or lost animals to her and she knew exactly what to do! Every child had a pet because Martha gave them one. I never dreamed I'd let a baby mongoose enter my house. And yet, we have the photo with Aunt Martha wearing oven mitts and putting a baby mongoose in the midst of a handful of MKs in our hallway! Only Martha could bring an iguana to prayer meeting in our house and get away with it.

"Though a doctor, Martha never lost sight of the Great Physician in her work. She recognized that the people she cared for were in far greater need than even they understood. Martha recognized that physical healing was just part of the full redemption story she wanted to share. She worked hard so that many would not only have life but also have it more abundantly.

"Many times I have sat in her presence at the ladies prison and listened as she shared in childlike terms what it means to choose Christ and how God seeks to draw all men to Himself. Often she would be examining someone in the jail and begin a Bible story. She could weave more stories together in 15 minutes and cover a great deal of biblical ground as she examined. The women would just sit around at her feet and I would note that what Martha was about was what Jesus was about when He walked the earth. You could feel and see His presence at work in her life, as she was Jesus Incarnate to those around her. She just could not help but speak what she knew to be the Way, Truth, and Life no more than she could refuse to physically help those in need. How easy it is to remember sitting among those women—telling jokes, sipping tea out of the one can we all shared, and touching their minds and bodies with her care.

"Reflecting back, Martha was simply there. When there was a journeyperson who came in, Martha took them out in the community to visit. In our international community, we knew Martha was more at home in Yemen than in the USA. If the opportunity came to visit with Martha, you wanted to take it. I learned much from watching her interact with the Yemenis. She was one of them. She was with her family. I recently received an email from one of my Yemeni Muslim friends in Jibla. She said when the tragedy occurred that took Martha, the entire country of Yemen was broken with sorrow because they lost one of their own.

"Then she added that she knew that every word Martha said was truth and that God was holding her hand even now in heaven. Even in her absence, the life of Martha Myers demands that every disciple of Christ take a closer look at the needy world and give of ourselves to meet their needs. It also cries out to the Yemeni people that she served to remember her Jesus and His message of hope."

Martha—through the eyes of Stephen Edwards

Author's note: Kidnapping of foreigners has become more common in Yemen the last few years. More than 200 have been held for ransom or had their cars stolen. Some kidnappers have even traded foreigners for jobs! While most are released unharmed, some have been hurt or killed. Kidnappers are usually quite successful. Keep those facts in mind, and marvel even more at how God worked in Martha's life as Stephen speaks!

"This is the story about Martha's kidnapping. Because Martha was so often on the road, it was not unusual not to hear from her for two or three days at a time. I realize how much we took God's grace for granted.

"My wife, Kandi, was the first person in Jibla that Martha contacted when she got free from the carjacking/kidnapping attempt. She was in Dhamar, a city halfway between Jibla and Sana'a. She had called from the police station, to the best of my recollection. Kandi continued to contact others of our group, and I and another of our men set off to Dhamar.

"What we found was so typically a Yemeni, and a 'Martha,' situation. We were introduced in stages to various levels of local and state officials, though it was impossible to distinguish rank or office, but we didn't find Martha. Eventually, we were ushered into the office of the governor of the state, once again indistinguishable by dress or pretense, and spent several hours with him. He was profoundly hospitable, and we realized after a time that we would have to follow the protocol if we ever hoped to be reunited with Martha. Late in the night (about 1:30 A.M.) Martha was brought over to his office.

"She had spent the latter part of the afternoon and evening with the governor's wife, and had been meeting family members and learning to cook Yemeni dishes and had been feted during this time in the most honored of fashions. As was always Martha's way, she had developed an instant rapport with this kind lady and made the lasting impression she always did, being received as one of the family. In the most adverse of circumstances, the grace of God was upon her and those around her were also blessed.

"After being reunited that night with Martha we spent quite a while beginning to say good-bye to our Yemeni hosts. We were all very desirous to get back on the road, and began the process of seeking information about the car Martha had been driving. We did not want to leave it on the road if at all possible. Even then I was not aware of how God had been watching over her. They had stayed on the main roads with her stuffed and covered in the small cargo area in the back floor.

"They hit a new unpainted and unmarked speed breaker, and immediately the car stalled. They were near a gasoline station, and tried in vain to restart the car for some 15 or 20 minutes. They finally gave up and abandoned both the car and Martha.

"Upon inspection that night we found that the bounce had jolted the car's distributor and thrown out the timing. Repair was simple. The miracle of it all was that this model of car is designed for the most brutal of use, and had probably endured countless bumps of this magnitude before without failure. The proximity of the car to the filling station was more evidence of God's providential care over her.

"But the lasting effects were profound. Once again Martha had been ushered into the presence of princes and kings, as it were, in the service of our King. Her grace had opened hearts in the highest hall of that state. God is good."

In the next chapter, you can learn from Martha herself all that happened during that harrowing afternoon, and how God was with her.

15
The Kidnapping

One of the miracles of this book is that Martha kept a journal of the kidnapping—in great detail. She typed it up and gave it to Joanna for safekeeping. Martha titled the report: "Surprise Attack from Bait Einan; a.k.a. One Busy Weekend!"

Martha had promised to meet the bus from Sana'a in Ibb to help a family with their post-op paraplegic baby and his 2-year-old brother and 4-year-old sister. She was driving Stephen Edwards's short-wheelbase Toyota. It had been in maintenance for some minor repairs. The windows were open and the doors were unlocked. Usually Martha drove a locked car and did not unlock doors while she was driving. Today, however, she was running late.

Arriving at the bus station, Martha discovered that the bus had broken down and they were repairing it. She decided to go to the broken-down bus. It was a beautiful late summer afternoon. She started singing "The Love of God." She had promised to sing it that night in church.

She started up the steep slopes of Sumara Mountain which had many sharp hairpin turns. She tried to pick up speed, but she was going uphill and on a curve so she was not fast. Suddenly, there were three fairly tall, slender, army-jacketed young men in the road, two in her lane and the third in the oncoming left lane, all with rifles drawn. She realized that there was a problem as the center man leveled his rifle at the car.

"No way," Martha thought. "We don't have hijackings in Ibb! Maybe in Sana'a or Marib!"

It was too late. The man in the middle of the road got in the car easily because all the doors were unlocked.

Martha asked, "Fi mishkila?" ("Is there a problem?") "Fi mishkila," ("There is a problem,") said the one who got in on the driver's side. Another man entered the car on her right and he pulled her from under the steering wheel by grabbing her by her arm. Martha resisted and her legs were still under the wheel as the new driver was taking off. A third man got in.

Martha conceded they were in and thanked God that in Yemen they don't usually kill those who are hijacked or kidnapped.

The man on her right had his face covered with his black-and-white mashadda. When he pulled Martha over from the driver's seat, her scarf, an important part of her modest dress, came off.

She asked repeatedly, "Almasar, almasar, ya, Habibi, wain almasar?" ("My scarf, my scarf, beloved, where's my scarf?") The third man, in the backseat, found it behind her and she put it back on.

There were oncoming cars and the men waited for them to pass and then ordered Martha to get in the back. The man in the right front seat took her glasses, then untied his mashadda, folded it, and wrapped it over her eyes, then tied it in back.

(Later when others talked of another vehicle, a red Nissan Patrol with Emirates license plate, Martha wondered if the blindfold was so she wouldn't see their accomplice car.)

They told her to lie down on the floor so she wouldn't be seen. Then the man in the back said, "Fi khof, fi mot." ("There's fear, there's death.")

Martha replied, "Ana ma akhof min almot, lianna eindama amot, sha'aruH ila aljinna." ("I'm not afraid to die, because when I die I will go to heaven.")

"Anti Muslima?" ("Are you Muslim?") asked one of the men in the front seat in surprise.

"Ani masiaHiya. Ani mu'mana fi tariq Aisa bin Mariam." ("I'm Christian, I believe in the way of the Christ, Isa, son of Mary.") Martha was not sure she finished the last sentence before they interrupted with "Shut up." She put it in the Lord's hands and was at peace.

If the men were to shoot her because she knew too much or if she should be shot in a cross fire, she would go to heaven. She reasoned she had had a nice career and been able to help some people. She was not too uncomfortable. In fact, if she folded her arm to cradle her head, she could take a nap! But then she could imagine her friends laughing at her sleeping during a hijacking.

The men discovered that petrol (gas) was getting low. Martha told them she had plenty of money in her brown bag. They found the money and her pager. She'd only had it 5 months. She told them to take out the battery, but they didn't understand. Martha slipped out the battery later under the blanket. She was afraid someone might call at a checkpoint and a battle would break out.

Before they stopped for gas, they stopped for a blanket to cover Martha. Someone in the front yelled, "Sura'a! Sura'a! Sura'a! Sura'a!" ("Quickly! Quickly! Quickly! Quickly!)" She didn't think they had time to go in and buy something, but they quickly covered her with a blanket. Had they grabbed it off a fence? It smelled clean, however, not dusty. It was pleasantly comfortable before the afternoon sun heated the car.

When they drove into the gas station both the men in front got out. The man in back cautioned Martha, "Wala haraka, wala kilma! Fi khof. Fi mot." ("Not a move, not a word! There's fear. There's death.")

The next 20 to 30 minutes were uneventful. Then they hit two speed bumps. But on the second one, the car stopped, and they couldn't get it started. The driver kept pumping the gas pedal. Martha wondered if he had flooded it. Finally they got the car off the road. They left after warning Martha to be quiet and not to move or "fi mot." ("There's death.")

Would they return? They did, with a bag of *qat* (the leaves that have a narcotic effect when chewed). The man who had been in back gave Martha a bottle half full of water. She drank some and poured a little on herself.

The men worked long and hard on the car, but couldn't revive it. Martha said she finally realized they did not want her—they wanted the car.

They left a second time with the same warnings. Martha slipped off the blindfold and looked at her watch. Without her glasses it was difficult. She finally made out 4:45. She had been held captive about three hours.

A few minutes later Martha heard a child say, "There's a lady in the car!" and another child said the same thing. Then a man said, "There's a lady in the car and the license plate is white!" A white plate meant imported, often belonging to a foreigner. They had figured it out, but the kids figured it out first!

Martha was worried that the hijackers might return. She waited 10 minutes, then emerged. A man came from a few yards away and said, "We knew you were in there, but we didn't know if you were dead or alive. We have called the Criminal Investigation."

Martha hesitated. The men had the key, but she got out and locked the car with the blanket inside. Across the road was a gas station with a phone. The station attendant allowed her to call even though she had no money. (Later she returned and thanked the attendant and paid him.)

She called Bill Koehn, the hospital administrator. The first thing Martha told Bill was to tell Kaye she wouldn't be there to sing at the service that night. Then she told him she had been hijacked and exactly where she was. She told him she'd call Stephen Edwards or Ron Nichols to come get her.

After that Martha answered questions of Criminal Investigation and then was taken to the governor's house. The governor was kind both officially and personally. He took Martha to his home and his wife offered her a change of clothes and bathing facilities. She was glad to wash up but declined the clothes.

Stephen and Ron arrived. They had been able to get the car started with the help of a mechanic. The points were off. They brought a spare key with them when they came.

All three of them thanked the governor for supper. He invited them to stay the night at his house, but they were eager to go home.

Martha spent the night at the hospital but went home the next morning for a bath and change of clothes. She was surprised to find bruises on her right arm, fingerprints of the man who had covered his face. There were also small scratches where his nails had dug in. Although she had not felt this the night before, Martha thought she needed this visual evidence to help her realize that the episode was not a nice little game.

Later that day Martha and the Jibla Baptist Hospital security officer went to see the director of security for Ibb. He assigned the hospital security officer to go over the scene of the hijacking with Martha. A representative from Criminal Investigation was assigned to go also.

At one of the stations the attendant told them there was a second car, a red and silver Nissan Patrol. Martha had not been aware of another car! Two men were in the Nissan, making a total of five hijackers.

Martha assisted the security forces but matters moved slowly. There were no developments for about six weeks. Eventually, all five were arrested.

In the end, three were released and two had their hands slapped.

All in all, it was an unhappy experience.

16
The Last Furlough

"For years Martha never took a furlough at all," says her father, Ira Myers. "She was too busy and too much in love with Yemen. In fact, she never ever took over 90 days at one time." He pauses then and adds—"until her last furlough."

Then he chuckles. "She'd hurry home, get her teeth fixed, and have a medical exam. Oh, yes, she'd keep up with missionaries all over the world. Our phone bill resembled the national debt!

"She bought videotapes by the gross and she'd duplicate tapes all night long. She'd buy out the bookstores. She had a book addiction!

"She spoke everywhere she was asked. She wanted people to know about Yemen.

"She spent every penny she had on people in need. Her last check cleaned out her bank account. It was for a 13-year-old Yemeni girl who needed a kidney transplant. 'Things don't matter,' she believed. 'People do.'"

Martha came home for another of her very brief furloughs to see her mother, who had had some serious health problems. Dorothy was diagnosed with pancreatic cancer shortly after Martha's arrival in 2000.

Dorothy was the last one in the world to insist on her daughter's staying home because of her. Again and again she'd remind Martha that Yemen was now her home and God's place for her.

The International Mission Board, however, insisted that Martha take a longer furlough to recover from the trauma. Some who recommended rest and counseling, had themselves actually been more traumatized by the incident than Martha. But Martha wrote concise reports and kept journals and served the Lord in every way she could as 14 long months crawled by.

God used her to disciple two young women to prepare them for kingdom service. Cheryl Blow and Pat Harris were both members of Dalraida Baptist Church, the Myers family's home church in Montgomery.

Martha—through the eyes of Cheryl Blow

When Cheryl first got to know Martha, she told her she had heard of Martha for years at Dalraida but never had the opportunity to meet her because she was so seldom there. She told Martha she was like an icon. Shocked, Martha gave her a slight smile. "Really?" She had no idea of how well thought of she was.

Cheryl admitted that she and Pat did not know Martha as long as most people, but that their time together was intense and during a difficult time in Martha's life. They became good friends.

Martha taught both Cheryl and Pat a lot about money. Martha used her money for the glory of God. They often ran errands together.

"I never saw her buy anything for herself other than necessities," claims Cheryl. "With one exception—books! She had a love for books! The books were nonfiction. She felt life is interesting enough to negate the need for fiction. I once saw her buy all six copies of a book the bookstore had on the difficult life of a Saudi Arabian princess. She gave these copies away so that women in America could understand the plight of women in the Middle East."

During Martha's 14-month stay in the US, she found she had not packed for a long furlough. She had to buy some clothing. She went to a used clothing store to make her purchases. She bought a pair of shoes at Kmart. Some of her clothes in Yemen came from yard sales.

"I saw Jesus in her," Cheryl declares. "When I read *The Mind of Christ* I saw in Martha the examples the book gave of how Jesus lived. Before knowing her, I would not have believed it possible for a human being, other than Jesus during His time on earth, to really live such as the book suggests, but Martha did! She would not say anything bad about anyone, even those who gave her difficulties.

"I learned from her not to be so critical of others. People were drawn to her and sensed that she truly cared about them. She was so understanding of people and their problems. I think Martha had a love for every person she met, and that love showed in her face and in her actions. When she smiled, you could see love oozing out of every pore!

"Martha totally surrendered herself to God. She knew she had to go back to Yemen. I made the remark, 'It's very noble of you to want to go back.' She promptly replied that she was not in Yemen to serve the International Mission Board. God had called her there."

Martha—through the eyes of Pat Harris

"I had met Martha several times before 2001 when she was sent home for what turned out to be an extended period of time. Since I became a member of Dalraida Baptist Church in Montgomery, Alabama, during the mid-1980s, Martha had been introduced on short visits home. It was not until her last extended visit home that Cheryl and I had the opportunity to really get to know her.

"It started when Cheryl invited Martha to visit the laboratory at Jackson Hospital where both of us work. She immediately demonstrated her quiet, soft-spoken words of wisdom. She was really drawn to the international staff, seeking out information with which she could relate. Everyone instantly was drawn to her as were Cheryl and I. Our friendship began to develop as she seemed to be reaching out to us and we loved her immediately. We went on walks almost every night and afterwards just sat and visited, talked about each other, and developed a deep friendship which was to last us our lifetimes. We enjoyed having a bowl of ice cream, which quickly grew to a ritual after our walks.

"Over those months Martha was here she immediately fell into a routine of serving God in Montgomery and around Alabama. Cheryl and I were included when she was going to speak and share about Yemen.

Martha and I took a course at Dalraida titled The Net, a program for an evangelism technique. "Several times we were together when we went out on visitations. She was gentle and simply shared her testimony with those we visited. Often she would ask Cheryl and me to go with her to visit. It was either someone she had met that was willing to hear more about Jesus and church, or it would be a shut-in to whom she would carry literature and visit. Martha became involved in sharing at the church with RAs, went on a youth retreat with teenagers, and shared as WMU asked her to speak all over Alabama.

"On our 'walkie-talkies' one night we could tell she was really missing Yemen. She really wanted to return and she felt that approval to return was taking a very long time. I said, 'Do you think the International Mission Board has something else in mind for you?' To which she answered, 'I know God has called me to serve Him in Yemen among the people there.'

"On one of our trips to a WMU group where she spoke, I noticed that she became emotional while she was sharing the things on her heart about her work in Yemen. As she closed you could hear the emotions in her prayer and weakness of her voice as she held herself together. It was at that moment I realized how very much that Martha was suffering because she was being kept from her calling of God to Yemen. She always talked to Cheryl and me about 'when ya'll come to Yemen to visit,' what she wanted to show us about the country and the people. She loved Yemen and the Yemeni people.

"Our hearts had become very attached to Martha and we were saddened to let her return to Yemen for our own selfish reasons, but knew how very happy she was to get back to God's work for her there. Her family encouraged her to return to Yemen. They were so unselfish.

"We were encouraged to come for a visit. Jolene Ivey, Cheryl, and I were to travel together in September 2002 to Yemen. About a month before we were to finalize the trip, Jolene had to back out due to health and personal family reasons. Cheryl and I decided to go as Martha assured us she would be there to meet us and travel with us while in the country. I kept telling Cheryl that this trip would change our lives! I did realize how God's hand was in this whole relationship, blessing and allowing it to grow for the three of us on a journey that would change our lives forever."

17
Praise God!
Back to Yemen

On September 11, 2001, terrorists used airplanes to strike at the United States, killing thousands of Americans and sending waves of fear to people of many countries. Travel, especially international travel, was heavily curtailed. Yet 3 months later, on December 11, 2001, Martha Myers left the US to return to Yemen.

Her life would also be taken by a terrorist. She had no idea how limited her time was—only 1 year plus 19 days. She had so much to do, so many Yemenis to visit, so many to share the Lord with. Only God knows how much she accomplished. However, a great deal can be glimpsed through the eyes of several workers who knew her well.

Martha—through the eyes of Mirjam (Miriam) den Dekker

"My name is Miriam; I'm a nurse from Holland. I went to Arabic countries and found out I loved it. I applied with a missions agency and they asked me if I wanted to go to Yemen. I had been in six countries in the Middle East, but had to look up Yemen on the map!

"I went and they sent me to Jibla Baptist Hospital. I loved it and the people. This was in January of 1998. I left in August of 1998. I did meet Martha and, like everybody else, I was impressed by the energy she had, always working, always visiting people, always talking about the Lord, always taking people out for trips, and (what impressed me the most) always smiling.

"I went home on furlough but returned in January of 2002. I looked for a house in Ibb. One was the house next to Martha. She was very enthusiastic! 'Yes, please be my neighbor!'

"But others advised me not to do it. They told me that she had psychological problems or that she was being watched by security or she was a bit strange. I told Martha that I was positive about the house, but I told her what people had said. She had tears in her eyes. 'You don't need to fear what the people say or fear the security police. We should fear the Lord!' Then I was sure I should rent that house, and it was the best decision!

"In the evenings Martha came knocking at my door. Often we talked for hours. She told me about the time she had to stay in the States. She didn't want to, she wanted to be back in Yemen. They made her get psychological help; she obeyed, with pain in her heart. The Lord assured her He wanted her to go back to Yemen and He provided a new visa and work permit to go back!

"She told me about the kidnapping and how she survived. She knew she was being watched by the security police. Our telephone lines were tapped. You always heard 'clicking' when we were calling or sometimes I heard Yemeni voices. Once I heard a Yemeni saying, 'It's the Dutch girl!'

"She knew every house, and when we were driving she'd say, 'That house is full of weapons' or 'that house is al-Qaida.'

"Martha and I just clicked. They were critical about Martha going out and picking up Yemeni men in her car who wanted to know more about Jesus! They couldn't come to her house— not appropriate in such a culture. So she handled it this way and still some Americans said it was wrong of her. When she told me this, she cried. But I was with her several times, and I am sure this was from the Lord. It was just a little church in the car!

"Every Tuesday a Yemeni girl who became a child of the Lord came to Martha's house. We studied the Bible together, prayed, and sang songs. Be sure, there is a hidden church over there and many became believers because of Martha!

"It was clear that all the Yemenis loved her. Even the one who killed her loved her because it was not possible to not see that she loved everybody!

"It was hard to see how painful it was for Martha when the Baptists decided to stop financing the hospital. Three people really hurt: Bill Koehn, Kathy Gariety, and Martha. How special it is that the Lord took just those three on to heaven! He knew they couldn't live on in Yemen with their love for the hospital, for the work.

"I just loved to have Martha as a sister/neighbor/mother/friend. I loved to go out with her visiting Yemenis. I loved to do Bible study with her with Yemenis. I loved to go vaccinating off-road. I loved to go on trips Sunday mornings very early and then to church. I loved to go to the prison with her, to go to weddings. I loved it when she came home late and knocked on my door and came talking.

"The last day the hospital was open I was going with Martha to clinic, but I woke with a terrible migraine. I planned to go at 10:00, but I got that phone call. There had been a shooting—Martha had died.

"I can still feel the pain in my stomach when I write this. But it's good to have the assurance that she's with the Lord now, singing the 'Hallelujah Chorus' forever."

Another influential person in Martha's life was also from Holland, a midwife, Thea [Tee-ah] Groenveld.

Martha—through the eyes of Thea

"My friendship with Martha was deep, God-centered, and Yemeni-centered. My first years living in Yemen, trying to learn the language, getting used to the new surroundings, there was little chance to hear something from outside and take it in. Yet, as there were times of prayer, sharing in our team, one name came up regularly: Dr. Martha. The reactions from some, when her name was mentioned, raised in me a certain degree of curiosity. Some would smile, others spoke of her with deep appreciation. What I did get was she loved people.

"After serving in the country for four years, I could travel down to Jibla Baptist Hospital for a week's holiday. This is an eight-hour journey.

The one who greatly encouraged me to go was my German colleague, a midwife and friend. She said, 'You won't be sorry.'

Martha was not well and we did not meet. After having a lovely week, I wrote her a short letter and pushed it under the door of her office.

"My next visit to the hospital was with my two older friends from my home country of Holland. On the day we arrived, Dr. Martha was out on a vaccinating trip. Though my two friends went to bed, the Lord put it on my heart to stay awake and wait for her return.

"At 11:00 P.M. the sound of a Land Cruiser broke the silence of the night. That would be Dr. Martha. I introduced myself and simply explained the reason to be there so late at night. 'I would like to pray with you.'

"No further explanation was given or asked for. She came and sat next to me, took my hands in hers, and we prayed, offering petitions for the land and rendering to the almighty God a song in the night.

"Further meetings with Martha would continue in such a simple, uncomplicated manner. I thanked God to meet this woman after His own heart. From then on, we were real friends, more than previously only knowing each other by pen and paper. To say it with Martha's own words, calling it kinship. I acknowledge such a meeting was arranged by the loving Father in heaven.

"Martha was called for a home visit. A security officer needed her to see his wife. This was not the first time. As she was talking to the man, I noticed an Arabic Bible. Then a friend of the security officer entered the room. He picked up the Bible and began leafing through the pages. I then heard the officer say: 'That is my personal Bible, you can take the other one.'

"I visited with Martha another security officer. I sensed that the wife and daughter were used to her presence. After breakfast, the man showed me his Bible. He told me, 'I am a believer but I cannot talk about it outside of my house.'

"Deeply grounded in God's word, living it out in simplicity, not ever forcing it on someone: her lifestyle spoke to the Yemenis. It still does."

Martha—through the eyes of Minnie Garrett

Minnie and her husband, Richard, were volunteers at Jibla Baptist Hospital until 2004.

"All at Jibla Baptist Hospital as well as many Yemenis were concerned about the future of the hospital. The International Mission Board had been trying to close the hospital for years. Bill Koehn had the word *Baptist* painted off the sign at the front of the hospital in an effort to convince the locals that the IMB was serious about walking away on January 1, 2003."

A group of retired doctors who had served under the Foreign Mission Board (now International Mission Board) worked feverishly trying to keep Jibla Baptist Hospital open. Time ran out.

On December 27, 2002, a contract missionary from Ireland told about a meal at the hospital for the Yemeni staff, past and present, and all internationals. The Yemenis were all very sad, she reported, "and there were tears. A lot of families will suffer from loss of jobs.

"The Yemeni charity that was supposed to receive the hospital admitted they couldn't take it. It will now be handed to the MOH (Ministry of Health) who say they can't run it. If they are willing to accept the Christian NGO (non-government organization) that has offered, there would be a lot of happy people. NGO is very clear in their statement of mission, which is medical care plus sharing the gospel. If MOH says yes, it will be most definitely the Lord's doing. The alternative will be MOH and their cohorts stripping the hospital and benefiting greatly from the spoils. That would be a sad end to a great service for the people and a significant chink for the gospel in this country."

Finally, the last day for the hospital to be open arrived: December 30, 2002. It was to be a full day. They would not close the doors until every patient had been seen.

At 8:00 A.M. everything changed.

18
In the Blood of Martyrs

The events of December 30, 2002, actually began an entire year earlier. In December 2001 Abed Abdel Razzak Kamel and his wife came to Jibla Baptist Hospital from north of the capital city of Sana'a for a medical consultation.

The couple saw an Indian contract doctor who referred them to Dr. Martha. She was out of the country at that time, but she saw them in January 2002 just after she returned.

According to the US State Department agent who interviewed Kamel, his wife was so impressed with Martha that she later told her husband that no Muslim doctor had ever treated her with such love and compassion. Kamel told the interviewer that if Dr. Martha could have that kind of impact on his wife after just one meeting, then he knew he "had to kill her" to keep her from spreading Christianity in Yemen.

Out of this man's hatred grew a plot to kill Martha and as many other Christian workers as he could at Jibla Baptist Hospital. (Further investigation showed that Kamel was part of an al-Qaida cell that killed a political leader in Sana'a just days before the murders in Jibla on December 30, 2002.)

Kamel originally intended to commit the crime on Christmas Day—his "gift" to the Christians. The hospital was closed for Christmas, however. He changed the date of the massacre to December 26. Car trouble prevented him from keeping this appointment.

Finally, he arrived on Monday, December 30, 2002.

Bill Koehn, Kathy Gariety, and Martha Myers's martyrdom was pieced together from eyewitness accounts and official investigations by Lee and Lisa Hixon, International Mission Board (IMB) missionaries.

The hospital gates opened at 6:00 A.M. on December 30. Abed Abdel Razzak Kamel entered Jibla Hospital with his return appointment card. He spent over two hours sitting on the bench by the x-ray department waiting for Martha.

At 8:15, presumably tired of waiting, Kamel paged her. Martha came into the clinic area, walked right by Kamel, and entered Bill's office to use the telephone—to answer the page by Kamel.

Bill Koehn, the hospital administrator, was in his office seated at his desk. Kathy Gariety, the purchasing agent for the hospital, was seated across from Bill. Kamel followed Martha into the outer office, outside Bill's office.

Bill's secretary, Amran, detained Kamel. He insisted on entering Bill's office, however, on the pretense of buying a phone card. When Amran tried again to stop him, Kamel pulled out his handgun. Then the shooting started.

He shot Martha twice as she stood by the phone returning Kamel's page. He then shot Bill twice. Then he turned the gun on Kathy, shooting her twice. All three were fatally wounded.

Kamel still had three bullets when he left the administrative office. He spotted Don Caswell, the missionary pharmacist, standing at the door of the pharmacy. When Don saw the gun, he stepped back into the pharmacy.

Kamel followed Don and fired his last three bullets. Don was struck twice.

As Kamel left the pharmacy he pointed and "clicked" his empty handgun at three other Christian workers in the clinic area. Within seconds of his leaving the pharmacy, soldiers surrounded Kamel and he surrendered.

Another who was eye witness to some of the events of that day was a contract doctor from Mexico, Sara Elena Perales Saldana. She and Martha met in 1996 when Sara arrived in Yemen. They became very close friends. Sara describes Martha as Jesus Christ's love in Yemen.

"Her love for the people was one of the most important things in her life. Her patients were her friends, not just her patients."

That fatal Monday, Sara awoke at 5:30 A.M. and decided not to go to chapel because she knew she would cry and cry. It would be the last chapel service before the government was to take over the hospital. Instead, she decided to go straight to the clinic. She arrived a little after 7:00 A.M. She knew Martha was in the room that she was usually in that day. Her supervisor had told Sara the day before that she should use the room next to the pharmacy.

Sara saw Kathy, who seemed very busy going to the store before going to Bill's office. Sara hurried into the hospital to pick up some medicines from Martha and Kathy to help the very poor patients. She returned to her room in the clinic, where some patients already waited outside while others were just arriving. She was seeing her first patient, a nurse from the hospital, when suddenly she heard shooting.

She told her patient, "Someone is shooting us! The shots are coming from Mr. Bill's office!" Then Sara heard shooting from next door—the pharmacy.

"Oh no! Don, the pharmacist, is dead—and he has children and a wife!" she cried.

The shooting stopped. The next door was Sara's door—which was open. But the killer did not come in. Sara went to the door and saw the killer putting the gun on the floor and lifting his arms.

Sara hurried into the pharmacy to help Don, who was still alive. She asked someone to call a surgeon, while she checked his wounds and then assured him that he would be OK. As soon as the surgeon arrived, Sara went to Bill's office.

The first thing she saw was Kathy being carried on a stretcher to the OR. She was still breathing, but Sara saw the blood on her chest and feared she would die soon. Then she saw Bill on his chair with a gunshot in one eye. Others were holding him up.

Sara put her stethoscope on his chest and heard his heart beating, but weakly. He was dying.

Then Sara saw Martha. She was still alive. Her eyes were open, but there was a shot through one of them. Sara cried, "Martha! Martha!" In the next few silent moments they both knew what was going to happen.

On Martha's face was a soft smile, the last one. She was going to see God, the One Who had led her to Yemen many years before.

A lot of people surrounded Sara and Martha, but Sara saw only Martha. Then she noticed a Yemeni whom Martha loved very much. Knowing he would also want to be close to Martha, she asked, "Please, can you take Dr. Martha and help put her on a stretcher?" Then she staggered out into the hospital to find a phone. She wanted to call one of the missionary families who lived out of the hospital compound—to tell them not to come to the hospital. Keep the children safe. She thought, "Martha loved the children so much. Keep the children safe."

News spread quickly in Jibla and around the world. A press release from the US State Department issued the same day as the murders read:

"The United States condemns the despicable attack on health workers at the Baptist Hospital in Jibla, Yemen early this morning that left three American citizens dead and another injured. There can be no justification for an attack such as this on an institution providing critical humanitarian services to the Yemeni people. We extend our deepest condolences to the victims, their families, and their loved ones. Personnel from the U.S. Embassy in Sana'a are in Jibla to assist at this very difficult time. The United States welcomes the arrest of a suspect earlier today by Yemeni authorities and we will be working closely with the Yemeni government to fully investigate this murderous attack."

An Associated Press release the day after the bloodbath proclaimed that townspeople gathered to mourn at the gates of the hospital, shut since the shooting.

Inside, two of the dead were buried in a missionary cemetery in the hospital compound. Dr. Martha Myers, 57, of Montgomery, Alabama, had worked in Yemen for 24 years. Hospital administrator William E. Koehn, 60, of Arlington, Texas, had planned to retire the next October after 28 years at the hospital.

The body of the third victim, Kathleen A. Gariety, 53, of Wauwatosa, Wisconsin, who had worked in Yemen for 10 years, was to be flown back to the United States.

"Today was very sad for all of us, and what made it even more sad was that we couldn't participate in the burial," said a Jibla resident who had worked in the hospital. "All Jibla weeps for them," she said, choking back tears.

Another woman, wearing a black veil that covered everything but her eyes, said Martha had treated her during her first pregnancy, when she was confined to her bed for months for fear she would lose the baby.

"Every day she looked after me, she used to come to my house, until I was able to stand and walk without endangering my pregnancy," she said, cradling her 2-year-old son in her arms.

"Without Dr. Martha, I wouldn't have Ali," she said. "She was a friend more than a doctor."

A student outside the hospital declared, "This is treachery of the highest form! Dr. Martha was like a mother to all of us and to all the residents of this province. Whoever committed this crime killed us all."

A storeowner in Jibla blasted the killer as an "inhumane murderer."

"This has been such a shock, a dreadful shock because the whole team were so good to us. No one from here would even consider doing this."

"Kamel did not take their lives; they chose to give their lives to Yemen long ago," said John Brady, the International Mission Board's regional leader for North Africa and the Middle East.

Yemeni hospital staff and friends built caskets for Bill and Martha, dug their graves, and lowered the bodies into the hard, rocky ground.

"This is my father," one of the Yemeni hospital workers said of Bill. "I have to do this."

The residents of Jibla were as devastated by the deaths as much as the Americans at the hospital, said Al Lindholm, another Southern Baptist worker. After spending a couple of days in prayer, mourning—and remembering—at Jibla, most Southern Baptist workers in Yemen traveled to Sana'a to rest, heal, and regroup.

One piece of good news at this time was that Don Caswell, the pharmacist, was in good condition and recovering from surgery.

Just days after the attack, it was made known that most of the workers had no plans to leave. Even Marty Koehn, Bill's widow, planned to stay to encourage the Yemeni people who were grieving the loss of her husband.

Lee Hixon, Bill's assistant, put it this way: "The call of Jesus Christ to take the gospel personally to hurting individuals far outweighs the risks of living in a country like Yemen."

If you had asked any of these three, "Would you give your life to birth the church?" they would have said, 'Absolutely.'"

In the blood of His saints, His church is born.

19
The Whole World
Wept

Not only Jibla wept—the whole world wept.

The International Mission Board notified the families of Martha Myers, Bill Koehn, and Kathy Gariety in the wee hours of the morning of January 1, 2003. Then word spread like wildfire from one end of the world to the other.

Those who called the Myers residence in Montgomery before dawn broke that morning heard Dorothy, who was then critically ill, say, "Martha beat me home!" (Five months after Martha was killed, Dorothy succumbed to pancreatic cancer and joined her daughter in heaven.)

Newspapers in every language covered the tragedy, as did television and radio broadcasts. Lee Hixon claims that more people were praying for Yemen and the remaining missionaries there than ever had before. "They were praying, 'Bring them home safely.' They should have been praying 'Stand them up and give them boldness to preach the gospel in that dark place.'"

Even the American Medical Association took note of Martha's death. In its online forum, amednews.com, an article titled "American MD Killed Serving Troubled Corner of the World" told of Martha's death, as well as of Bill's and Kathy's. Besides giving an outline of Martha's life and work, the article emphasized the needs she was meeting in Yemen: 1 in 13 Yemeni women die in childbirth; polio had been reported as recently as 1999; 62 children out of 1,000 die before their first birthday; only 12 percent of women give birth in health-care facilities.

One of the ways she was described in the article was as a woman who went to medical school "driven by Christian faith and a desire to help people."

In Yemen and in many places in America memorial services were held for the slain missionaries. Tributes were given, memories were shared. Families were flooded with telegrams, emails and letters.

On January 30, 2003, Bill O'Brien, former vice-president of the Foreign Mission Board (now International Mission Board) delivered the following memorial at Martha's alma mater, Samford University (formerly Howard College).

Had she been anyone else her epitaph might have read:

> Martha Myers
> 57 years old
> Graduated from Samford University
> OB/GYN doctor in Yemen for 24 years
> Cause of death: gunshot wound to the head

A more compassionate journalist might have listed the cause of death by saying: "Dr. Myers's life was taken by a terrorist's bullet."

The truth of the matter is that Dr. Martha's life was not taken. She had long since given it away. It started at First Baptist Church of Avondale, Georgia, where she made her profession of faith. You could call it "a long obedience in the same direction." Her life was centered in the person of Jesus Christ. With an undivided heart she gave herself to the Yemeni people.

She would say, "Things don't matter—people do." And the people of Yemen knew that, especially the women and children. Whether in the hospital or traveling the dusty roads of the villages, Dr. Martha brought the contagion of hope to the hopeless. She emptied herself. Her expertise, her smile, her money, her friendship—all were means of revealing that she loved God with all her heart, mind, and soul, and her neighbor as herself. And you couldn't tell when she was loving God and when she was loving the Yemeni people. It was all the same.

When Nelson Mandela was released from prison, he was accompanied to the heart of Capetown where 500,000 fellow South Africans awaited him in the town plaza. He appeared on the balcony of a building and spoke in measured tones. At the close of his remarks he made a profound statement: "The rest of my life I place in your hands." Only time would tell if he meant what he said. And he proved it.

She may have never said it just the way Mandela did, but Dr. Martha lived it. For she knew she couldn't place the rest of her life in the hands of God without placing it in the hands of the people for whom He died.

After a visit to Yemen, a friend wrote about her:

"She could practice medicine out of her four-wheel-drive Land Cruiser as easily as an American doctor might order drugs from a stainless steel dispensary. She could change flats as easily as she could change diapers in neonatal. Her hands were equally firm with the scalpel and the tire tool. She could read both x-rays and four-wheel-drive repair manuals. God was on the throne. Many would be converted. Some would live and some would die, but life could not be so extreme as to make her fear. There was work to do. Christ would enable her to get His work done, and there is no other work worthy of being done."

Today her body is at rest on the grounds of the hospital—proof that whether in life or in death she would never be far from the people she loved, nor from the Master she served. And the Master said, "Inasmuch as you have done it unto one of the least of these, you have done it unto me. . . . Well done, good and faithful servant."

Martha's influence continues all over Yemen—and beyond. Thea, the Dutch midwife and Martha's good friend, tells about "Jane" whose life was changed dramatically.

Jane and her husband live in the northeast of Yemen where they both grew up. Now they are in a happier situation than 11 years ago. The person who was an instrument to change their misery and pain into praise and gladness was Dr. Martha.

Thea got to know Jane in a small outpost clinic where she had begun to do a clinic every two weeks. The place was deserted. Though of recent construction, it had no running water or electricity.

"Two of us worked there: an ophthalmic nurse and myself, a midwife. We met many precious people there. One of them was Jane. She had not only suffered much from her condition but also at the hands of many physicians. Her problem was a fistula due to prolonged child-birth. Her first and only child was stillborn and she became incontinent. A damaged bladder made her an unclean woman. She had a loving husband, who had not divorced her, as is usually the case.

"As Jane came to our clinic, we heard her story. Five times she had surgery in Saudi Arabia. Between them were long periods. None were successful. It is a difficult operation, which only a few can perform.

"Martha came to mind immediately. But after all those surgeries there would be much scar tissue and this makes another attempt extremely difficult."

Thea talked to Martha by phone. She agreed to operate. Jane and her husband made the long nine-hour journey to Jibla. They went with real trust. Knowing they were going to a Christian hospital only strengthened their hope for healing.

They didn't worry about finances. Believers from Thea's circle of friends had helped in this. Her brother, who had visited Yemen just a week before, had donated blood. (He didn't even mind, in the minutes after he donated, that he fainted on the Jibla stairs.)

Everything was ready.

Aware of the immense request laid on Martha, Thea asked the Lord to give them a confirmation to undergird her in prayer. The Father gave them this verse which Thea passed on to Martha: "Heal me, O Lord, and I will be healed; save me and I will be saved, for you are my praise" (Jer. 17:14).

The operation went well and a fully recovered Jane went back to her village. Word began to spread.

"I can still recall the joy on both faces as we received them in our house. Soon after, I left the area. Only the Lord knows what has been the influence on that whole district, so far away and unreached, as it bordered Saudi Arabia. We knew that we could trust Jane to spread the word and to leave it to the Father to move the hearts of those who heard."

A missionary in Yemen shared about her Yemeni friend, "Laura."

"Laura was a dear friend and had been for 3 years. She had had previous contact with many of the foreigners living in Jibla and nearby Ibb. I was amazed to hear that Martha had patiently loved Laura, despite her sometimes unkind and ungrateful behavior. I learned of this as I was sharing the good news of salvation with her. I must have been quite passionate as I spoke, because she had a very serious look on her face. But I realized soon after what that look meant: she interrupted me to say, "Jesus is the son of God."

"I looked at her, not believing at first what I was hearing. As I began to speak again, she interrupted again, saying, 'Did you hear me? Jesus is the son of God!'

"I was overjoyed! I asked her, 'Are you a Christian?' When she answered yes, I hugged her tightly. She was overwhelmed with emotion, saying, 'I have never told another person about my decision. You can't tell anyone!' I asked her to tell me her testimony."

Laura told her story: "I was unable to carry children. I would become pregnant but then lose each baby after a few months. Dr. Martha treated me, and I was able to have children. I now have several!

"Then I needed a hysterectomy. Dr. Martha performed the surgery. But I was in a lot of pain and very angry about everything. I had a husband who treated me poorly, not providing any money for food or clothes and beating me often. I would go to the hospital and yell and scream at Dr. Martha and Mr. Bill, but they were never angry with me. I acted awful but they never turned me away.

"Dr. Martha came to my home once in a while. One day she gave me the New Testament on tape because I can't read. I would sneak into my room by myself, lock the door, and listen to the tapes. As I was walking down the road one day, thinking about all that was happening in my life, I realized that what the foreigners said was the truth. Jesus was the Son of God. But I've never told anyone until today."

The missionary continued the story. "I could see the freedom she was experiencing in those moments. And that day began her spiritual growth. We would pray together sometimes when she would visit me, and I would share Scripture when possible.

"When Martha, Bill, and Kathy were martyred, she grieved deeply for them. She was unable to believe it had happened at first, just as several others explained their shock that day. And she was greatly burdened with the knowledge that she never told Martha—the one person who had done so much for her—of her faith in Christ. She would mention this almost every time that she came to visit me, until one day her tears stopped. She began telling me of a dream that she had had the night before, and as I listened, I realized that the Lord had answered her heart's greatest need."

Laura said, "I had a dream last night and I saw Martha. She was sitting in a beautiful room. It was so beautiful, I can't even describe it. She had food around her and everything that she could need. She said to me, 'Laura, why are you crying? I am in heaven and I have all that I need. But I am sad that you are crying. God will take care of you! And even though you never told me on earth, here in heaven I know that you are my sister.'"

These stories have been repeated over and over. During the funerals after the shootings, one Yemeni said, "Something is happening in my heart."

God is working in the hearts of people. The harvest is beginning. Not half has been told. Keep reading!

Epilogue

Meanwhile, in Yemen many things were happening—had been happening. Lee Hixon tells a story he says is a typical example of how Martha poured out her life in Yemen for the people God gave her to love.

One morning three weeks before the shootings, a Yemeni employee gave Lee a little bag of homemade cookies. These cookies are more like hard biscuits with very little sugar—an acquired taste. Lee knew Martha rarely ate breakfast before rounds and she liked these "eid" cookies.

He found her at the bedside of a patient—a young man who had tried to commit suicide. Martha was holding his hand and trying to share intently with him. Lee tried to slip the cookies into her lab coat pocket without disturbing the conversation but Martha said over her shoulder, "He says he's one of us, Lee!" Martha then made arrangements for Lee to give "Adam" a New Testament at a later time.

A couple of weeks later Adam met with Lee, expressing a great interest in the Christian faith. He eagerly accepted the gift of an Arabic New Testament. On that same day Martha made arrangements for him to see the *Jesus* film at Lee and Lisa's house the next day.

Martha planned to come just at the end of the film after she finished her rounds at the hospital.

She arrived at the close of the gospel presentation at the end of the film. Then she gently, lovingly led Adam in a prayer to receive Christ.

"We all rejoiced to see the transformation from despair to hope in this young man. This is just one example of how Martha touched lives. Time after time we saw Him working through her to bring healing not only to bodies but to hearts as well.

"If this story could be printed in Arabic, I know that Yemenis would stand up and say, 'Martha told me about Jesus, too!' In fact, it's a story we hear every day.

"We heard the story on January 5, 2003, when 30 or so international workers, including Bill Koehn's widow, Marty, walked the streets of Jibla seeking to comfort and finding ourselves comforted. The people of Jibla came up to us grieving and hurting. Many people said of Bill, 'He was like my father.'

"Others remembered Kathy's gifts of clothes and toys to sick children and their families. The refrain about Martha went like this, 'She was our mother.'

"In many ways, Martha's witness continues in the lives and in the testimonies of people she touched. We must say the same for Bill and Kathy as well. Their love is remembered and their compassion has not been forgotten.

"As for Martha, she looked to heal the whole person—we never knew her not to consider the eternal in any encounter. It is a privilege to have known her and a joy to see the lasting and continuing fruit of her labor of love. There are many here in Yemen who look forward to the day when they will see Him—and Martha—once again."

After the shootings, the hospital closed. Those who remained did not know their fate or that of the hospital. On February 1, 2003, however, Jibla Peace Hospital opened. Lee Hixon, the new administrator, reports they are seeing in excess of 150 patients daily, which accounts for 50,000 annually.

In the ancestral home of Osama bin Laden, the gospel is spreading. Something is happening in peoples' hearts. A great price was paid and that tragic day shook us and challenged us. It still does, says Lee Hixon.

confer matue #
146315 on phone

Payed up *$13.60* **Thank you!**

Your purchase of this book and other WMU products supports the mission and ministries of WMU. To find more great resources, visit our online store at www.wmustore.com or talk with one of our friendly customer service representatives at 1-800-968-7301.

WMU®
Discover the Joy of Missions^SM
www.wmu.com

52 5/98
Pony Pal

Pdon Bill
$73.60